VOICE AND PHENOMENON

Northwestern University
Studies in Phenomenology
and
Existential Philosophy

VOICE AND PHENOMENON

Introduction to the Problem of the Sign in Husserl's Phenomenology

Jacques Derrida

Translated from the French by Leonard Lawlor

Northwestern University Press
Evanston, Illinois

Northwestern University Press
www.nupress.northwestern.edu

Printed in the United States of America

10 9 8 7 6 5 4 3

Library of Congress Cataloging-in-Publication Data

Derrida, Jacques.
    [Voix et le phénomène. English]
    Voice and phenomenon : introduction to the problem of the sign in Husserl's phenomenology / Jacques Derrida ; translated from the French by Leonard Lawlor.
        p. cm. — (Northwestern University studies in phenomenology and existential philosophy)
    "Originally published in French under the title La voix et le phénomène by Presses Universitaires de France, 1967"—T.p. verso.
    Includes bibliographical references and index.
    ISBN 978-0-8101-2765-4 (pbk. : alk. paper)
    1. Husserl, Edmund, 1859–1938. 2. Phenomenology. 3. Signs and symbols. 4. Meaning (Philosophy) 5. Difference (Philosophy) I. Lawlor, Leonard, 1954– II. Title. III. Series: Northwestern University studies in phenomenology & existential philosophy.
    B3279.H94D3813 2011
    142.7—dc22

                                                    2011012609

Contents

Acknowledgments

While what I have produced counts as a new translation of Derrida's 1967 *La voix et le phénomène,* it is profoundly indebted to David Allison and to his original 1973 English translation, which appeared under the title *Speech and Phenomena.* Professor Allison trained me at Stony Brook University, and his English translation helped train a generation of Anglophone philosophers in Derrida's thought. It is hard for me to express the extent of my gratitude toward David B. Allison. I must thank Ronald Bruzina, who carefully read the first draft of this translation and gave me countless invaluable suggestions for revisions. Elizabeth Rottenberg also advised me concerning a variety of translation problems. Thanks are also due to Joe Balay, Aaron Krempa, and Cameron O'Mara at Penn State University who read later drafts; Daniel Palumbo assisted in the proofreading and indexing. I am especially grateful to Anthony Steinbock for his suggestions regarding the translation and for his support of the entire project.

Translator's Introduction: The Germinal Structure of Derrida's Thought

Published in 1967, when Derrida was thirty-seven years old, *Voice and Phenomenon*[1] appeared at the same moment as *Of Grammatology*[2] and *Writing and Difference*.[3] All three books announced the new philosophical project called "deconstruction." Although Derrida would later regret the fate of the term "deconstruction,"[4] he would use it throughout his career to define his own thinking. While *Writing and Difference* collects essays written over a ten-year period on diverse figures and topics, and while *Of Grammatology* aims its deconstruction at "the age of Rousseau," *Voice and Phenomenon* shows deconstruction engaged with the most important philosophical movement of the last hundred years: phenomenology.[5] Only in relation to phenomenology is it possible to measure the importance of deconstruction. Only in relation to Husserl's philosophy is it possible to understand the novelty of Derrida's thinking. *Voice and Phenomenon* therefore may be the best introduction to Derrida's thought in general. It is possible to say of it what Derrida says of Husserl's *Logical Investigations*. *Voice and Phenomenon* contains "the germinal structure" of Derrida's entire thought (3).

The structure involves three features (which are presented in the three sections of this introduction). First, and this is the most obvious feature, Derrida's thought is structured around the concept of deconstruction. But the concept of deconstruction can be determined only in relation to what it criticizes: "the metaphysics of presence." The metaphysics of presence is a closed system, determining the concept of sign (and more generally language) as derivative, as a modification of presence and having no other purpose than representing presence. Starting with presence and ending with presence, metaphysics forms a circular enclosure. Second, Derrida's thought is structured by classical forms of argumentation, in particular, by the investigation of unacknowledged presuppositions. But it is also structured by the invention of new concepts: différance, the trace (or writing), and supplementarity. Reconceiving the sign (or more generally language), these unclassical concepts are defined by impossible propositions, which, when deposited into the metaphysical system, stop the circle from being formed. They attempt to open the enclosure of metaphysics. Therefore, third, like so much of the French philosophy developed in the 1960s,[6] Derrida's thought is structured by an exiting movement, a line of flight to the outside. That the outside is a sort of utopian non-place, an "elsewhere," in which it is possible to think and live differently, indicates what motivates deconstruction. As we shall see, there are two motivations for deconstruction, motivations which one might find surprising if one is familiar with the way Derrida's thought was appropriated and popularized during his own lifetime. Derrida's thought is motivated by the desire for truth and for the transformation of all values. Undoubtedly, these are new concepts of truth and value, but they are truth and value nevertheless.

First Structural Feature: The Deconstruction of Phenomenology as the Metaphysics of Presence

None of the 1967 books, including *Voice and Phenomenon,* provides a formal definition of deconstruction.[7] But soon after, Derrida formulated one. In the 1971 interview "Positions," Derrida states that deconstruction consists of two phases.[8] The first, which is critical, attacks the classical oppositions that structure philosophy. These oppositions, Derrida states, are subordinating; they are hierarchies.[9] The first phase of deconstruction "reverses" the hierarchies. In order to reverse, Derrida focuses on the presuppositions of the superior term's authority. Under scrutiny, it turns out that the superior term presupposes traits found in the subordinate term. The sharing of traits points to a necessary structure at the base of the hierarchy itself. So, a second phase aims at marking the basic necessary structure; it aims at marking the relation, the difference or hiatus that made the hierarchical opposition possible in the first place (for Derrida's use of the word "hiatus," see 18).[10] The basic necessary structure is the "last court of appeal" (8), the law for the "distribution" of the terms or ideas found in the oppositions (13). Yet, the necessary structure is aporetical insofar as it cannot be determined by the terms in the hierarchical opposition it makes possible. Indeed, the necessary structure is so basic, so fundamental, so transcendental—Derrida calls it "ultra-transcendental" (13)—that it cannot be named properly or adequately; all names selected to designate it will have been determined by the very oppositions and hierarchies that the structure conditioned or generated. Nevertheless, Derrida will name the structure by means of what he calls "paleonyms," that is, with old names inherited from these oppositions and hierarchies.[11] In his reutilization of these names, Derrida aims "at the emergence of a new 'concept,' a concept that no longer lets itself, and has never let itself be included in the previous regime."[12] Therefore, while deconstruction's first phase operates on the terrain of the philosophical oppositions being reversed since the subordinate term holds the position of superiority in the same hierarchy, the second phase, through these new concepts (which are also new ways of thinking and living), aims to move beyond and exit the terrain of the philosophical opposition.[13]

Even though it does not explicitly formulate this definition of deconstruction, *Voice and Phenomenon* operates on the basis of the two phases of reversal internal to the terrain and on new concept emergence with the aim of exiting the terrain. While working through phenomenology in general, *Voice and Phenomenon*'s deconstruction specifically targets Husserl's early *Logical Investigations* (1900–1901), and in particular the First Logical Investigation. Derrida selects the First Logical Investigation because it concerns the sign as a means of access to the ideal meanings of logic. *Voice and Phenomenon*'s subtitle is, of course, "Introduction to the Problem of the Sign in Husserl's Phenomenology." The problem of the sign comes from the fact, as Husserl recognizes in the First Investigation, that there is an ambiguity in the notion of the sign.[14] Sometimes, Husserl notices, signs function to indicate a factual state of affairs, while at other times they function to express an ideal meaning. This intertwining of the indicative function with the expressive function is especially evident in communication (17). Husserl therefore attempts to make an "essential distinction" within this intertwining. Husserl wants to disentangle expression from indication, exclude indication from expression. Expression seems to present, while indication, an indicative sign, merely manifests something absent. Because expression presents, Husserl valorizes it over indication; only expression gives us access to ideal meanings. So, in *Voice and Phenomenon,* the deconstruction works first by Derrida reversing the hierarchy between expression and indication (18). Using argumentation internal to phenomenology, he shows that the indicative function, in particular, the trait of one thing being in the place of another, makes expression possible. In the indicative function of "being in place of," Derrida sees an irreducible repeatability. Repeatability is the necessary structure prior to the hierarchical opposition of expression and indication. Repeatability is that to which the new concepts or the new names of "différance," "trace" (or "writing"), and "supplementarity" refer; all three of these concepts, being prior to and beyond the opposition between expression and indication, point to an "elsewhere" of phenomenology (53).

Derrida develops the new concepts of différance, trace (or writing), and supplementarity, however, not in relation to the hierarchy located merely within Husserl's phenomenology, but in relation to a hierarchy that determines Western metaphysics in general, the hierarchy of presence over the sign. Husserl's philosophy belongs to "*the* philosophy" (44), it belongs to what Derrida calls "the metaphysics of presence" (22). The phrase "the metaphysics of presence" has been the locus of much controversy insofar as it seems to homogenize the history of Western philosophy. Nevertheless the application of the phrase seems to be justified. Using the term in its Kantian sense, Derrida speaks of "schemas" of metaphysics, outlines that allow the general concept of metaphysics to be unified with the empirical events of the history of Western philosophy. Despite the diversity of its events, Western philosophy exhibits schemas such as the substance-attributes relation, where substance is the present being which the attributes modify; or the subject-object opposition, where the subject is presence and the object is relative to the subject (72 note). Derrida is especially interested in the schema of derivation (44). In Husserl's phenomenology and in Western metaphysics in general, language, and in particular the sign, are conceived as being derived from perception or thought, that is, from intuitive presence or self-presence—as if perception and thought were independent of the sign, as if the sign somehow supervened upon perception or thought as a kind of accident.[15] Making the sign derivative opens the way for it to be conceived merely as a modification of presence or as merely relative to presence (44).

The general concept of metaphysics to which these schemas refer is complicated. It first of all involves a decision. Metaphysics is based on a decision about how to answer the question of what the sign and more generally language is. As Derrida says, "how to justify . . . the *decision* which subordinates a reflection on the sign to a logic?" (7, Derrida's emphasis). The decision seems to be justified on the basis of the knowledge we have of ourselves in the clarity of self-presence; it is based on the foundation, as in Descartes, of the "I am," the foundation of subjectivity and consciousness (46). Therefore in metaphysics, because we seem to know who we are, because we seem to be present to ourselves, because we seem *to be* present, we *desire* the same, presence and self-presence (89).[16] Like the decision from which it flows, this desire, which values nothing other than presence, also defines the metaphysics of presence. The desire must be fulfilled. On the basis of Derrida's translation of Husserl's German term "Bedeutung" (meaning) as "vouloir-dire" (rendered in this translation occasionally as "wanting-to-say"), it is clear that voluntarism, "voluntaristic metaphysics," is at issue (29). The fulfillment of the desire for presence then is brought about by the will, understood as the faculty that calculates means and ends. Motivated by the desire for presence, the will wills the means which lead to the end or purpose of presence. The means are a technology of the sign, the "technical mastery" of the sign (65). Techniques of speaking and writing (especially phonetic writing [69]) master the sign insofar as they reduce, eliminate, and purify the sign of any aspect of it which potentially contributes to equivocity or obscurity; the purification results in the sign being as univocal and diaphanous as the sound of my own voice (66 for diaphaneity, 80 for univocity). In other words, the technology attempts to limit the sense of the sign (and that of re-presentation and repetition) so that the sign functions as nothing more than a detour through which presence returns to itself. The metaphysical will wants that the potencies of repetition be limited to those of saving presence (43 for saving presence; 65 for potencies). Limiting the potencies of repetition to presence (limiting to what Derrida, following Husserl, calls "the relation to the object" [84]),[17] repetition is always bent back into the circle of an enclosure. Metaphysics is a closed system; the metaphysics of presence is, as Derrida says, "the closure of metaphysics" (44).[18] Closure means that the founding axiom or principle contains in advance deductively the final conclusion or consequence so that no new possibility appears as one moves from proposition to proposition within the system.[19] If no un-implied possibility supervenes on the system, then it is possible to live within the security of presence and proximity. The limitation therefore amounts to thinking and living within the security of the answer—the only answer given so far—to the question of the meaning of being: presence.

We can recapitulate the general concept of metaphysics in this way. The general concept (which is schematized onto particular historical events of Western philosophy) includes *five traits:* decision, desire, will, closure, and security. *First,* it includes a decision as to how to answer the question of the meaning of being. That answer is presence. *Second,* from that answer, a desire flows, a desire for presence. *Third,* in order to fulfill the desire, the will is required. The will wills certain means to the purpose of fulfilling the desire. *Fourth,* the willing of these means (techniques aiming at mastering repetition) makes a circle: what was intended at the beginning is found at the end. Metaphysics is a closed system; it is an enclosure. So, *fifth,* there is security within the enclosure. We might even say, as Derrida would, that within the enclosure life is not risked; contamination, disease, death, foreignness, and alterity, all of these have been pushed to the outside. Yet, *in truth,* is the enclosure this secure? And if truthfully the enclosure is porous, must we not change the meaning of *who we are?* We shall return to these questions in the third section.

As the phrase "the metaphysics of presence" indicates, what is at the center of Derrida's concept of metaphysics is presence. What is presence? Presence is first and foremost the *content* of an intuition. Being the content of an intuition means that presence is defined as what is available "in front of" my eyes or look. In metaphysics, the principal meaning of being is "being-in-front"; Derrida uses the phrase "être-devant," in which we can see the word "pres-ence," the Latin "prae" (before) + "esse" (being) (64). Being is what is before, nearby, and proximate and therefore what is without distance or hiatus. The content of an intuition, however, is diverse and changing. So secondly, presence means the *form* that remains the same throughout the diversity of content. This dual definition of presence is synonymous, Derrida asserts, with "the founding opposition of metaphysics": potentiality (intuitive content) and actuality (formal idea) (53; see also 6). To conceive, however, the actual formal idea as otherworldly is Platonism, "conventional Platonism" (45); it is, as Husserl would say, to fall into "degenerate metaphysics." In contrast, "authentic metaphysics" for Husserl conceives the ideal form (ideality)— "the authentic mode of ideality" (5)—as a repeatable form in which the diverse content will always appear, to infinity. As Derrida says, "presence has always been and will always be, to infinity, the form in which . . . the infinite diversity of contents will be produced" (6). Husserl determines being, then, not only as what is in front but also as ideality (45–46), not only "being-in-front," but also "ideal-being" (65). With these two senses of being, Husserl recognizes (as Hegel does) that form must be filled with content, that the form must be *lived.* But Husserl also recognizes that the repeatability "to infinity" of the form is never given as such (87). The repeatability of the form is always that of the indefinite (87). The indefiniteness of the repeatable form implies that intuitive presence will always be incomplete and non-full; there will always be more content. But for Husserl, the lack of intuitive fullness is only pro-visional (83). In other words, whenever presence is not full, whenever it is threatened with non-presence due to the ever-changing content, presence is posited as a *telos.* Presence was full and close by in the past and it will be full and close by in the future. "Being" (presence) is the first and last word of metaphysics, whether what is at issue is "degenerate metaphysics" or "authentic metaphysics."

We are on the verge of examining the second structural feature of Derrida's thinking, the argumentation used in *Voice and Phenomenon*

in particular and in deconstruction in general. But before we turn to
that argumentation, we should note one aspect of deconstruction that
we had not seen before: deconstruction aims to break out of the closure of metaphysics by interrupting metaphysics' circular movement. As
we have seen, deconstruction first reverses the oppositional hierarchy of
presence and the sign (or more locally, in Husserl, reverses the oppositional hierarchy of expression and indication). In the reversal (in the
first phase of deconstruction), the subordinate term, the sign, becomes
the principal term. Because the most general sense of the sign is "being-
for" or "being-in-place-of" (21), the sign coincides with re-presentation.
What has then become foundational in the reversal is a term determined
by and found within metaphysics: "representation" (38 note). But making
representation foundational means that the "re-" of the re-presentation
is no longer a modification supervening on a simple presence. The "re-"
of repetition precedes what is repeated, precedes perception or intuitive
presence, precedes form or idea, so that everything seems to begin with
re-presentation (38 note). More precisely, the phase of reversal results
in the subordinate term being reconceived. We have now passed to the
second phase of deconstruction. In the second phase re-presentation has
been reconceived in a way that is *contradictory*. The "re-" of re-presentation
necessarily makes the repetition be a second or a supplement; the "re-"
seems to make all representations and signs nothing more than modifications of something given beforehand, something like a model. But
insofar as repetition (through the reversal) is foundational, it is also or
at once a first or an origin. It becomes, as the oxymoronic title of chapter 7 says, "an originative supplement." As we move from the first phase
of deconstruction to the second, we have remained within the system of
metaphysics since we are still using the name "representation." But we
have also "deposited" *within* the system "contradictory or untenable propositions" (49 note), impossible propositions such as "everything begins
with representation"; "the second is first"; "the origin is a supplement."
These impossible or absurd, even false propositions provide the conceptual core of différance, the trace (or writing), and, as we see here, supplementarity. Done from within a certain inside of the system (within the
hierarchy of presence over the sign), the depositing of these aporetical
propositions and unclassical concepts interrupts the circular movement
and "opens [the closure of metaphysics] to its outside" (49 note). The
contradictory propositions open the system because they do not function as pointing to an object or to a subject, to a form or to a content;
they point to nothing that could be present as such. They point beyond
presence.

Second Structural Feature: The Basic
Argumentation for the Reversal of the
Hierarchy of Presence over the Sign

In general, the argumentation in *Voice and Phenomenon* demonstrates the
lack of cognitive foundation, that is, the lack of self-presence, for the
security of the metaphysical decision. More specifically, one finds three
overlapping arguments in consecutive order in chapters 4, 5, and 6. As
we have seen, in the First Logical Investigation, in order to gain access
to ideal meanings, Husserl wants to separate expression from indication.
He thinks he can find expression in its pure state when communication
with others has been suspended, in other words, in interior monologue,
"in the solitary life of the soul." Derrida tells us that, in order to support
the demonstration of indication being separate from expression in interior monologue, Husserl appeals to two types of arguments (41).

　　Voice and Phenomenon's chapter 4 concerns Husserl's first type of
argument. Here is Derrida's summary of it:

> In internal discourse, I communicate nothing to myself. I indicate noth-
> ing to myself. I can at most imagine myself doing that, I can merely
> represent myself as manifesting something to myself. Here we have only
> a *representation* and an *imagination*. (41)

As we can see from this quote, the first argument revolves around the role
that representation plays in language. In interior monologue, it looks as
though one does not really communicate anything to oneself; it seems
as though one merely imagines or represents oneself as a speaking and
communicating subject. For Derrida, this claim is problematic because
Husserl uses the word "representation" in many senses: representation
as the locus of ideality in general (*Vorstellung*); representation as repetition or reproduction of presentation (*Vergegenwärtigung* as modifying *Gegenwärtigung*); and finally representation as taking the place of another
Vorstellung (*Repräsentation*) (42). On the one hand, therefore, it seems as
though Husserl applies to language the fundamental distinction—"an
essential distinction," "a simple exteriority"—between reality as factuality and representation as ideality (representation in the sense of *Vorstellung*) (42). The distinction seems to imply, according to Derrida, that
representation as ideality is neither essential nor constitutive but merely
an accident contingently adding itself to the actual or factual practice of
discourse. But, as Derrida points out, when I actually use words, that is,
when I consider signs in general, without any concern for the purpose
of communication, "I must from the outset operate (in) a structure of

repetition whose element can only be representative" (42). Derrida says, "A phoneme or grapheme is necessarily always other, to a certain extent, each time that it is presented in a procedure or a perception, but it can function as a sign and as language in general only if a formal identity allows it to be reissued and to be recognized" (43). In other words, the sign in general must be an empirical event—"necessarily always other"—and it must be repeatable—"formal identity." This definition of the sign—a sign consists in a minimally iterable form—means that actual language is just as representative or imaginary as imaginary language and that imaginary or representative language is just as actual as actual language. Whether representative—"I think that I'm speaking when I speak to myself" (*Je me représente que je parle quand je me parle*)—or actual—"I am actually speaking when I speak to someone else" (*Je parle effectivement quand je parle à quelqu'un d'autre*)—the sign in general is re-presentational. On the other hand, if it is the case that when I speak to myself I am only imagining myself doing so, only thinking I am doing so (*je me représente*), then it seems as though my interior monologue is worked over by fiction (48). If this is so, then it seems that the consciousness in interior monologue is determined entirely as false consciousness (49). The access to the epistemological grounds of logic then seems jeopardized. But there is a further problem with representation. According to Derrida, Husserl in the phenomenological method has privileged fiction, the fiction of imagination; by means of imaginative variation, one is able to neutralize the existence of a thing and thereby generate an ideality (47). But Husserl's conception of "neutrality modification" never calls into question the determination of the image as a representation in the sense of *Vergegenwärtigung*, that is, in the sense of a representation that refers to something non-present. In other words, in interior monologue, the sense of representation appropriate to indication seems necessary for expression—just as in actual communication the sense of representation appropriate to expression seems necessary to indication. The iterability of the sign (repeatability, or re-presentation in all senses), therefore, casts doubt on Husserl's attempt to distinguish essentially between imagined speech as in interior monologue and actual or empirical speech as in communication, in short, between expression and indication.

Voice and Phenomenon's chapter 5 concerns Husserl's second type of argument to demonstrate that expression can be separated from indication in interior monologue. Here is Derrida's summary of it:

> In internal discourse, I communicate nothing to myself and I can only pretend to, *because I have no need to communicate anything to myself.* Such an operation—communication from self to self—cannot take place

because it would make no sense. And it would make no sense because it would have *no purpose*. The existence of psychical acts does not have to be indicated (recall that only an existence can in general be indicated) because the existence of psychical acts is immediately present to the subject in the present instant. (41, Derrida's emphasis)

According to Husserl, since lived-experience seems to be immediately self-present in the mode of certitude and absolute necessity, signs are useless, that is, the manifestation of the self to the self through the delegation of an indicative sign is superfluous. There is no need for or purpose to indicative signs here, since there seems to be no alterity, no difference in the identity of presence as self-presence. Because Husserl says (in the First Logical Investigation, §8) that "the acts in question are lived by us at that very instant [*im selben Augenblick,* literally, "in the blink of an eye"]" (cited in 41), Derrida claims that Husserl's immediate self-presence has to depend on the present taken as a now and that dependence on the now leads Derrida to investigate Husserl's *Phenomenology of Internal Time-Consciousness* (51). These descriptions of internal time consciousness attempt to describe the experience of time (temporalization), but especially the experience of the present as I live it right now: the living present. As Derrida reads it, *The Phenomenology of Internal Time-Consciousness,* on the one hand, indicates that the living present seems to have a *center* which is the now point. But, on the other hand, the time lectures indicate that the living present seems to be *thick;* it includes the immediate memory (called the retention) of the now that has just elapsed and the anticipation (called the protention) of the now that is about to appear. For Husserl, the retentional phase is different from memory in the usual sense, which he calls secondary memory; the usual sense of memory is defined by representation (*Vergegenwärtigung*). Because of the thickness, what is at issue, for Derrida, is precisely the kind of difference that one can establish between the retentional phase of the living present and secondary memory. In other words, what is at stake is the kind of difference we can establish between *Gegenwärtigung* and *Vergegenwärtigung,* between presentation and re-presentation. While Husserl shows in *The Phenomenology of Internal Time-Consciousness* the irreducibility of *Vergegenwärtigung* to *Gegenwärtigung,* Derrida nevertheless interrogates—without questioning the demonstrative validity of this distinction—"the evidentiary soil and the *milieu* of these distinctions, . . . [that is] what relates the terms distinguished to one another and constitutes the very possibility of the *comparison*" (55, Derrida's emphasis). It is important to recognize that Derrida is not claiming that there is no difference between retention and secondary memory (or *Vergegenwärtigung*). Instead, because Husserl in §16 calls retention a "non-perception," Derrida argues that there must be a *continuity* between retention and secondary memory such that it is impossible to claim that there is a *radical discontinuity* or a *radical difference* between retention and re-presentation; and therefore because the living present is thick, because the now cannot be separated from retention, there must be no radical difference between re-presentation and presentation or between non-perception and perception (55). As Derrida says,

> As soon as we admit this continuity of the now and the non-now, of perception and non-perception in the zone of originarity that is common to originary impression and to retention, we welcome the other into the self-identity of the *Augenblick*, non-presence and non-evidentness into the *blink of an eye of the instant*. There is a duration to the blink of an eye and the duration closes the eye. This alterity is even the condition of presence, of presentation, and therefore of *Vorstellung* in general, prior to all the dissociations which could be produced there. (56)

Within the duration, there is an alterity, a heterogeneity between perception and non-perception which is *also* a continuity. Between retention and re-production, there is only a difference between two modifications of non-perception (56). Therefore, as Derrida concludes, the alterity of the blink of the eye "cuts into, at its roots," the argument concerning the uselessness of the sign in the self-relation (57).

We have been considering the argumentation found in chapters 4 and 5, but the heart of *Voice and Phenomenon* lies in chapter 6. Chapter 6 concerns the voice of the title *Voice and Phenomenon*, the voice in interior monologue. For Husserl, according to Derrida—here Derrida relies on Husserl's description in *Ideas I* §124[20]—sense (a thought) is generated from a stratum of silence, "the absolute silence of the self-relation" (59). Sense must be generated as an object repeatable to infinity (a universality) and yet remain close by to the acts of repetition (proximity). In other words, sense must be simultaneously present in the sense of an object (the relation to the ob-ject as over and against) and present in the sense of the subject (the proximity to self in identity, as close as possible), both ideal-being and being-in-front together. In order for this to happen, a specific medium or element of expression is needed; that medium or element is the voice (65). Sense is going to be generated by means of hearing-oneself-speak, by means of this specific kind of auto-affection (67). In effect, Derrida provides a phenomenological description of hearing-oneself-speak. Here are the basic features of that description. When I speak silently to myself, I do not make any sounds go out through my mouth. Although I do not make sounds through my mouth when I speak silently to myself, I make use of phonic complexes, that is, I make use of the forms of words or signs of a natural language. The use of natural phonic forms seems to imply that my interior monologue is an actual (not ideal) discourse. Because, however, the medium of the voice is temporal—the phonic forms are iterated across moments—the silent vocalization endows the phonic forms with ideality (66). Thanks to the phonic forms utilized in hearing-oneself-speak, one exteriorizes the ideal sense (a thought). This exteriorization—ex-pression—seems to imply that we have now moved from time to space. But, since the sound is heard by the subject during the time he is speaking, what is expressed seems to be in absolute proximity to its speaker, "within the absolute proximity of its present" (65), "absolutely close to me" (66). The subject lets himself be affected by the signifier, but apparently without any detour through exteriority or through the world, or, as Derrida says, apparently without any detour through "the non-proper in general" (67); the subject seems to hear his *own* voice. Hearing-oneself-speak seems to be an absolutely pure auto-affection (68). What makes hearing-oneself-speak seem to be a pure auto-affection, according to Derrida, is that it seems to "be nothing other than the absolute reduction of space in general" (68). This apparent absolute reduction of space in general is why hearing-oneself-speak is so appropriate for universality (68). Requiring the intervention of no surface in the world, the voice is an "absolutely available signifying substance" (68). Its transmission or iteration encounters no obstacles or limits. The signified or what I want to say seems to be so close to the signifier that the signifier seems to be "diaphanous" (69). Yet the diaphaneity of the voice is only apparent since, now reverting back to the argumentation found in chapter 5, it is conditioned by temporalization. Temporalization indeed makes the voice ideal, but by doing so it also makes the voice (the phonic forms) repeatable to infinity and therefore beyond the acts of expression taking place right now. As repeatable, the phonic forms have the possibility of not being close by. They are able to function as referring to something (intuitive content) that is still to come; they are able to refer to non-presence, which turns the voice into an opaque murmur. In other words, the phonic forms are able to function indicatively—within the silence of expression. So, even in the auto-affection of hearing-oneself-speak, we find that we are not able to exclude indication, to separate it out from its entanglement with expression.

These three arguments—the argument from representation (chapter 4); the argument from temporalization (chapter 5); and the argument from the medium of hearing-oneself-speak (auto-affection) (chapter 6)—operate on the local terrain of Husserl's phenomenology. But they also operate on the larger terrain of metaphysics in general. We see this expansion if we recall that since Plato's *Theaetetus* (189e–190a) thought has always been defined as interior monologue, as the auto-affection of hearing-oneself-speak. The larger terrain of metaphysics is the ultimate transcendental level. Indeed, when Husserl describes the movement of temporalization, he recognizes that he is describing the level from which the sense of all things and experiences derives. He calls this level "the unnameable" (72 note). It is this unnameable and ultra-transcendental movement that Derrida (that deconstruction) is attempting to name. Derrida's conception of this movement is indebted to one phenomenological insight: the insight that Husserl discovers in the Fifth Cartesian Meditation. Indeed, perhaps all of Derrida's thought flows from this insight. Husserl brings to light that the experience of others (what he calls "Fremderfahrung," the experience of the alien) is always mediated by a *Vergegenwärtigung*, a re-presentation, which keeps the interior life of others necessarily hidden from me (6). What Derrida is doing throughout *Voice and Phenomenon* (and perhaps throughout all of his writings) is generalizing the sense of the non-presence of others to all experience, even to my own and proper interior experience of myself. For Derrida, all auto-affection is in truth hetero-affection. Generalized *Vergegenwärtigung* is at the root of all the new names Derrida develops for the ultimate transcendental level, for the movement of temporalization: "différance," "trace" (or "writing"), and "supplementarity."[21]

Let us see how these names evolve out of the movement of temporalization. In the living present there is a process of *differentiation* that produces the phases of the now, retention, and protention; the process of differentiation also includes repetition (the retentional phase) that allows for an identity to be produced and recognized. In other words, if we think of interior monologue, we see that a difference between hearer and speaker is necessary, we see that dialogue comes first. But through that dialogue (the iteration of the back and forth) the same, a self, is produced (71). And yet the process of dialogue, differentiation-repetition, never completes itself in identity; the movement continues to go beyond to infinity so that identity is always *deferred*, always a step beyond.[22] "Différance" names this inseparable movement (what we called repeatability above) of differentiation and deferral (75).[23] We can see how "trace" comes about if we focus on the feature of deferral, repeatability to infinity. The retentional phase of the living present retains the intuitive presence that has just elapsed. It retains, however, not its presence but only the outline of the presence, as if the retention were a *tracing* of it. The retentional trace then seems to be a remainder from the past, like a trace left behind by some living, but now absent, being. Let us continue with the idea of deferral to infinity. The trace refers back to this absence, but it continues to come back and function. The trace really resembles a memory. Insofar as it continues to function as a memory does, it also resembles something *written* (an outline, a drawing, a tracing), and Derrida indeed calls the movement of temporalization "archi-writing" (73). The repeatability to infinity of the retentional trace, which defers the final institution of an identity, is like a book, a book always available for other readers and therefore for other readings. The name of "supplementarity" evolves out of the written book always available for other readings. The "book" seems to be produced by someone who had certain thoughts present to himself, thoughts that he may have externalized in speech to others. But since human thought is finite—the author and his interlocutors have died— the "book" refers to that living but now dead author; it functions as a reminder of those thoughts that were present in the past. It seems then that the voice that keeps silent (self-present thought) is *first,* and *then* we have expression in speech, *and then* we have speech being written down. In this sequence, it looks as though writing comes *third.* It seems as though writing could never be "archi." But the truth is that a movement of "writing" or "tracing" comes prior to the voice. As we have already noted in the discussion of hearing-oneself-speak, the movement of temporalization in truth constitutes ideal meaning, constitutes presence. We have already spoken of the originative supplement. But now we see that what defines the supplement for Derrida is a paradoxical structure in which the very movement that produces presence comes to be seen as derived from that which the movement makes possible (75–76). Although writing in the sense of differentiation-repetition makes presence possible, writing in the everyday sense (a book) seems to be derived from the presence of thought; writing seems to be a mere supplement. As a supplement, writing is taken back into the terrain of metaphysics.

Third Structural Feature (and Conclusion): The Two Motivations for Deconstruction

The deconstruction enacted in *Voice and Phenomenon* takes place on four different but interconnected terrains. First, as we have seen, it operates on the terrain of Husserl's phenomenology. Derrida directs the deconstruction against the "essential distinction" between expression and indication which Husserl makes within the ambiguity of the sign. Husserl wants this essential distinction to be radical, a difference of separation, exclusion, and exteriority. He believes that he finds pure expression in interior monologue because, in interior monologue, my thoughts seem to be present to me at the very instant that I say them. In other words, Husserl thinks that when I speak to myself, the meaning of what I say is immediately present to me. Derrida shows, however, that Husserl's own descriptions of the experience of time (temporalization) demonstrate that in the present as I live it right now there is still and always mediation and representation. So Husserl's arguments for the immediate self-presence of expression in interior monologue are false. In fact, the living present is contaminated with non-presence, with the non-presence of the trace. Having dissimulated this contamination, phenomenology is therefore a form of "the metaphysics of presence."

The phrase "the metaphysics of presence" brings us to a second terrain, larger and deeper, more fundamental than phenomenology: the terrain of metaphysics. As for Heidegger in *Being and Time*, for Derrida in *Voice and Phenomenon*, presence has determined the meaning of being in the history of metaphysics since the ancient Greeks and right up to Husserl's phenomenology.[24] Presence is defined as that which is available in front of my look; it is what is proximate, the content of an intuition. But the content of an intuition is changing and diverse, which means that presence must also be the permanence of a form or idea. It is possible to conceive the permanence of the form or idea as otherworldly, in the heavens. Such a conception is Platonism or "degenerate metaphysics." Phenomenology, in contrast, conceives formal presence (ideality) as that which is to be lived; as lived, the form does not fall from the sky. Husserlian phenomenology therefore is a form of *anti-Platonism;* it looks to be a way of exiting metaphysics. For phenomenology in general, one overcomes metaphysics only by means of the unification of intuition and idea, of content and form, of actuality and potentiality, of subject and substance. But even when phenomenology recognizes that the unification is indefinitely deferred, it conceives that deferral as a history—the only concept of history—at the end of which the unification will occur. Whenever presence is not full or impure, whenever it is threatened with non-presence, presence is posited as a *telos.* Presence remains the principal and ultimate value. Therefore, even though it tries to change terrain, phenomenology remains within the terrain of metaphysics.

The question of exiting metaphysics brings us to the third terrain on which the *Voice and Phenomenon* deconstruction takes place: the border of metaphysics. *Voice and Phenomenon* puts the systematic solidarity of certain phenomenological concepts to the test (85). Phenomenology must be put to the test, because phenomenology seems to involve two movements. On the one hand, through the concepts of sense, ideality, objectivity, intuition, perception, and expression, phenomenology seems to *belong to* metaphysics insofar as metaphysics constructs a system of concepts whose "common matrix" is oriented by the value of presence (85). On the other hand, phenomenology seems to contest itself from within; by means of the concepts and descriptions of temporalization and alterity (*Vergegenwärtigung*), phenomenology seems also *not to belong* to metaphysics. In this second movement of contestation, phenomenology is a movement *toward* the outside of metaphysics. The phenomenological reduction, more precisely, the epochē, opens up the first and perhaps only way to exit metaphysics. Therefore, phenomenology presents for Derrida as it did for Heidegger an original kind of thinking, perhaps the first original thinking since Plato and Aristotle. We can see this tension within phenomenology by focusing on the book's title. The book's title—*Voice and Phenomenon*—reverses the roots of the word "phenomeno-logy"—*logos* (voice as the element of the *logos*) and *phainomenon* (presence as what defines the phenomenon).[25] The reversal means that instead of the *phainomenon* of the *logos* being valued, now, with deconstruction, the *logos* of the *phainomenon* is valued. But it is not the *logos* understood as the diaphaneity of the voice. What is valued is the *logos* as the resource of representation, mediation, and non-presence, as all the potencies of repetition.

The phenomenological contestation of metaphysics brings us to the fourth terrain, which we have named several times already: the outside. For Derrida who follows what Husserl says explicitly in *The Crisis of European Sciences*, the Greek metaphysical tradition, in which the meaning of being is defined by presence, finds its completion, 2,000 years later, in phenomenology (5). It finds its completion and its overcoming. Although it cannot be stressed enough that "the primary intention and distant horizon" of *Voice and Phenomenon* does *not* consist in turning back away from transcendental phenomenology (38 note), and that *Voice and Phenomenon* and Derrida's thought in general is a form of transcendental philosophy, one must recognize the radicality of its project.[26] Like transcendental phenomenology itself, the project of *Voice and Phenomenon* consists in going back to the roots of the knowledge of objects, but it goes back to roots deeper than those found by phenomenology itself, roots beyond those found in the Greek metaphysical tradition. It goes back to or beyond to, as we already mentioned, the ultra-transcendental. Although it is Derrida's central, most important book on Husserl's philosophy, *Voice and Phenomenon* is more than a book about phenomenology and its relation to metaphysics. The new names that it invents—"différance," "trace" (or "writing"), and "supplementarity"—form a "common matrix" as in metaphysics, but the deconstructive matrix is *not* oriented by the value of presence. Not oriented by the value of presence, this matrix or terrain, this plane or land, is not an enclosure. It looks like no place that has ever been inhabited before. When one engages in a deconstruction, one is dismantling in the name of this unnameable place.[27]

The phrase "in the name of" leads to one last elaboration. Why should we want to exit the system of metaphysics? There are two motives for Derrida's deconstruction of the general system of metaphysics (of which Husserl's phenomenology, in *Voice and Phenomenon*, is the specific historical event). First, what motivates Derrida is a concern with truth. We have seen that the belief that presence comes first and its repetition comes second, that belief is false. That presence comes first is only "apparent" (see 66, where Derrida says that the "transcendence [of the voice] is only apparent"). The truth is that there is a necessary structure that includes within itself opposing and inseparable possibilities and forces (it is the law): event and repetition, proximity and distance. This truth is even the truth of phenomenology (26). Even though the necessary structure—ultra-transcendental, unnameable, even undeconstructible[28]—includes the in-adequation of the forces of event and repetition, even though it therefore includes dis-adequation and non-truth, this "falsehood" is the truth dissimulated below the axioms and principles of Western metaphysics (and religion [88]) (46 note).[29]

The second motive for deconstruction is deeply connected to the motivation of truth. By means of the argumentation we have seen (especially the argumentation from the medium of hearing-oneself-speak), deconstruction demonstrates that the self-knowledge of the "I am" is only apparent. The lack of cognitive foundation allows deconstruction to unmake the metaphysical decision for presence. In other words, it reopens the question of the meaning of being. Or, more precisely, deconstruction aims at hearing the question in a new way, in asking an "unheard-of question" (88).[30] Hearing the question in an unheard-of way makes us recognize that this question has no one absolute answer, that every answer given to it is inadequate, that every answer will find itself opposed by another possible answer. Hearing the question in an unheard-of way is supposed to make us exit the enclosure and experience the *insecurity* of the question. Although Derrida does not use this word in *Voice and Phenomenon*, the insecurity toward which deconstruction aims to lead us is the experience of *undecidability*.[31] For Derrida, the experience of undecidability is supposed to make us *think* differently. Thinking differently means that whenever an answer to the question has been positioned, thereby closing off the question with an object or an objective, it is necessary to open the question back up, to speak out and speak freely (see 76, where Derrida refers to "the freedom of language, the outspokenness of a discourse"). In other words, in the face of the recognition that there is no one absolute answer to the question, we must seek constantly, endlessly, for the right answer. Seeking the right answer, or better, the *just* answer implies that the experience of undecidability is also supposed to make us *live* differently. The experience is supposed to call forth a new collectivity, a new people, a new *demos,* a new "we." We must abandon the metaphysical desire for presence and abandon the will to the mastery of repetition. Because the truth is that repetition comes first and that it comes last (which means that there is no unified origin and that there is no final end), prior to and beyond presence (which means that the first and last word is *not* "being"), because the truth is "the confession of a mortal" (47), we must—this "must" refers to the *force of law*—let the *delimitation* of repetition happen, with all its possible yet to come events. The source of insecurity in truth lies in that we do not know what event is coming. We must risk our lives in the face of contamination, disease, death, foreignness, and alterity. Abandoning the metaphysical desire and will, we must "value" non-presence (even though the word "value" here makes no sense, since how can one value that about which one does not know?). Therefore we can say that what is really at stake in *Voice and Phenomenon* is something like what Nietzsche called the "transvaluation of all values."

Translator's Note

Here are several points a reader should know about this translation. I have ordered them roughly according to the order that the reader will encounter them.

1. The numbers in angle brackets < > correspond to the page numbers of the French edition of *La voix et le phénomène* (Paris: Presses Universitaires de France, 1967). My own interjections in the body of the translation or in Derrida's notes are also enclosed by angle brackets.

2. Derrida's notes are placed in footnotes, while my additional notes appear as endnotes. Many of the endnotes, as in chapter 3, for instance, provide full citations for quotations which Derrida omitted.

3. In general, in order to make the English translation of *La voix et le phénomène* as seamless as possible, I have almost always modified all the existing English translations cited. This includes not only the *Logical Investigations* but also Fred Kersten's English translation of Husserl's *Ideen zu einer reinen Phänomenologie und phänomenologischen Philosophie: Erstes Buch,* James Churchill's English translation of Husserl's *Vorlesungen zur Phänomenologie des inneren Zeitbewusstsein,* and Roy Harris's translation of Saussure's *Course in General Linguistics.* Even though I have almost always modified and sometimes completely retranslated (appropriating wording from the French translations) the quotations from these English translations, I have provided the page references to the existing English translation so that the reader will be able to find the equivalent passage and the context of the quotations.

4. Almost immediately in the introduction (5), Derrida refers to the ontological distinctions Husserl makes in *Ideas I* (§96–97) between "real" in the sense of something factual and transcendent to consciousness; "reelle" (here Derrida uses the French word "réelle") in the sense of a part of consciousness, immanent to consciousness; and "irreelle" (here Derrida uses the French word "irréelle") in the sense of something ideal but not factual and not a part of consciousness, an immanent transcendence. The Kersten English translation renders "reelle" as

"really inherent" and "irreelle" as "really non-inherent." In order clearly to signal these differences throughout the translation, I am rendering "real" as "real"; "reelle" and "réelle" as "reell"; and "irreelle" and "irréelle" as "irreell." Derrida has also discussed these ontological differences in his " 'Genèse et structure' et la phénoménologie," in *L'écriture et la différence*, 242–44; " 'Genesis and Structure' and Phenomenology," in *Writing and Difference*, 162–64.

5. If one looks at note 11 in the introduction (found on 96), one will see that Derrida says that "each time that we shall cite this translation, we shall indicate this by the signs 'tr. fr.'" He then goes on to say that he has replaced in the French translation the word "significations" by *"Bedeutungen."* This comment implies that when Derrida does *not* use the sign "tr. fr.," he is not using the available translation and instead is translating the *Logische Untersuchungen* himself into French. The infrequency of this sign ("tr. fr.") implies that throughout *Voice and Phenomenon,* Derrida is making his own French translations of *Logische Untersuchungen.* Consequently, I have almost always modified the citations from J. N. Findlay's English translation of Husserl's *Logical Investigations* (which itself has been revised by Dermot Moran) in order to make them more consistent with Derrida's French translation and with the available French translation of the *Logische Untersuchungen.* I have also used the sign "tr. fr." in order to indicate the few times when Derrida seems to be relying on the available French translation of the *Logische Untersuchungen.*

6. I have relied on the earlier James Churchill version of Husserl's *Phenomenology of Internal Time-Consciousness* since Derrida relies on the Henri Dussort French translation (*Leçons pour une phénoménologie de la conscience intime du temps*). The Churchill English translation and the Dussort French translation are based on Edmund Husserl, *Vorlesungen zur Phänomenologie des inneren Zeitbewußtseins.* The Husserliana volume of these lectures appeared only in 1966: *Zur Phänomenologie des inneren Zeitbewußtsein, 1893–1977,* Husserliana X. I have consulted John Brough's more recent English translation of Husserliana X: *On the Phenomenology of the Consciousness of Internal Time.*

7. Derrida's insertions of Husserl's German and Derrida's interpretative comments within Husserl's quotes are signaled by square brackets.

8. I am rendering "instance" as "instance" or "case" and sometimes as "court" (p. 8, for example) or "agency" (13 and 60); at other times, where the term seems more idiomatic, I render it as "in the last analysis" (5, 9, and 61). Derrida's use of the term "instance" seems at times to be based on its use in Freudian discourse. In reference to the term "instance," one should examine the entry on "agency" in Laplanche and Pontalis's *The Language of Psychoanalysis.* Laplanche and

Pontalis say, "when Freud introduces the term 'agency'—literally 'instance,' understood in a sense, as Strachey notes, 'similar to that in which the word occurs in the phrase "a Court of the First Instance" '—he introduces it by analogy with tribunals or authorities which judge what may or may not pass" (Laplanche and Pontalis, *Vocabulaire de la psychanalyse,* 202; *The Language of Psychoanalysis,* 16). Derrida's use of the term "instance" also alludes to that of Lacan in his "L'instance de la lettre dans l'inconscient ou la raison depuis Freud" (originally published in 1957), since Derrida says, in the 1971 interview "Positions," that he had read this article prior to the publication of his earliest text on Freud, "Freud and the Scene of Writing" (originally published in 1966). See Jacques Lacan, "L'instance de la lettre dans l'inconscient ou la raison depuis Freud," in *Écrits,* 493–528; "The Instance of the Letter in the Unconscious, or Reason Since Freud, in *Écrits: The First Complete Edition in English,* 412–43. See also Derrida's long note on Lacan in *Positions,* 112n33; *Positions,* 107n44.

9. I am rendering "recouvrir" and the words based on this verb primarily by means of "coincidence." So, for instance in the introduction, when Derrida is speaking of the parallel relation between phenomenological psychology and transcendental phenomenology, he speaks of "ce recouvrement parfait," which I have rendered as "this perfect coincidence." The reader, however, should keep in mind that the French term also means to conceal, to cover over, to hide, and to overlap with. So one could also say that, in the parallel relation, psychological experience is the concealment (*recouvrement*) of transcendental experience. Sometimes I have therefore rendered "recouvrir" as "to hide."

10. Derrida renders Husserl's "Anzeichen" into French as "indice." This French word presents a difficulty since it means both indication and index. Chapter 7 takes up precisely the question of what an index or indexical is. So I have generally rendered "indice" into English as "indication," but at times depending on context, I have rendered it as "indexical," as in chapter 3 when Derrida is speaking of the solitude of the self-relation.

11. The variety of words used to refer to meaning present a complicated problem, as indicated already in note 4 above. Derrida at times uses "signification" to render Husserl's "Bedeutung." When he is doing this, I have used the English "signification." But then he renders "Bedeutung" by the French "vouloir-dire." I have rendered Derrida's use of "vouloir-dire," when he uses it to translate Husserl's "Bedeutung," by the normal English rendering of both the French and the German, that is, as "meaning." The French title of chapter 3 is "Le vouloir-dire comme soliloque"; the French title of chapter 4 is "Le vouloir-dire et

la représentation." However, it is important to keep in mind that Derrida deliberately renders "Bedeutung" as "vouloir-dire," since one of his themes in *Voice and Phenomenon* is voluntarism. The voluntarism or the will is implied by the French verb "*vouloir* dire," if one stresses the "vouloir" of the term "vouloir dire"—although the use of "vouloir dire" in French is equivalent to the English "I mean" ("je voulais dire" equals "I meant"). Often, in order to indicate that "vouloir dire" implies voluntarism, I have inserted the French verb "vouloir dire" in angle brackets. At other times, in the context of animation and the will, I have rendered it literally as "wanting to say." I have generally rendered the French "sens"—which renders the German "Sinn"—in English as "sense," even though both "sens" and "Sinn" refer to meaning.

12. The reader of this translation should also keep in mind the theme of possession, which is announced by means of the French word "appartenance" (here rendered as forms of the verb "to belong") at the close of the first chapter ("marque l'*appartenance* de la phénoménologie à l'ontologie classique": "indicates that phenomenology *belongs* to classical ontology").

13. The theme of possession (what is one's own, what is proper to oneself) continues through the use of "propre" (here rendered at times as "one's own" and at other times as "proper," depending on context). Derrida uses the French word "propre" to render Husserl's uses of "eigen" (in English, "one's own" or "proper") and "Eigenheit" ("ownness") as found in his Fifth Cartesian Meditation.

14. The theme of possession is connected to the theme of taking. The verb "prendre" and its past participles appear frequently. The first time a form of the verb "prendre" appears in a systematic way is at the end of the introduction: "une prise." Here, "une prise" has been rendered as "a grip." Where it seems that Derrida is using forms of prendre in a systematic way (to refer both to the idea of a belonging and to contamination), I have rendered it as a form of "grip." The important locations are in the first chapter and at the very end of the seventh chapter. The reader should also bear in mind that the French verb "comprendre"—related to the French verb "prendre," to take—means both to understand and to be included in. So, at the very end of chapter 7, when Derrida is speaking of the Teniers painting, he says that "this situation is not comprehended [*comprise*] between intuitions and presentations," meaning that it is not caught between, grasped, taken in and included, held between these two presences, and so it cannot be understood in terms of these two presences. Moreover, when Derrida uses the term "reprise," for example in relation to the idea of the dialectic at the end of chapter 5, I have rendered it as "resumption." This term, however, also has a sense of "taking up."

15. Findlay renders "kundgebende Funktion" as "intimating function." I am, however, following the French translation, which uses forms of the word "manifestation."

16. Findlay renders the title "Die Ausdrücke im einsamen Seelenleben" as "Expressions in Solitary Life." Derrida renders it as "Les expressions dans la vie solitaire de l'âme," which I have rendered here as "Expressions in the Solitary Life of the Soul."

17. I have rendered the French "motif" as "motive," since Derrida uses the term in the sense of what motivates to action, a reason or a cause for action. The term is connected to "motivation," to "motor," and to "impulse." The term also has the sense of "pattern," as in the motif of a melody (the recurring figure or theme).

18. As one sees in the concluding section of chapter 7, the distinction between "en fait" and "en droit" is important. I have rendered this distinction as "in fact" and "in principle." The word "droit," however, has a juridical sense of law or right, as in "the right to expression," as seen in chapter 1.

19. I have rendered "effectivement" as "actually," and "en effet" as "actually," while rendering "actuellement" sometimes as "currently" and sometimes as "actually right now."

20. Derrida makes use of a typographical artifice in the word "représentation" in order to indicate when the term refers to Husserl's term *Vergegenwärtigung;* in this case Derrida inserts a hyphen after the "re": "re-présentation." The hyphenated version of the term also translates Husserl's *Repräsentation.* When the term appears without the hyphen ("representation"), it refers to *Vorstellung.* I have reproduced this artifice in the English translation.

21. In chapter 7, when Derrida is speaking of the relation of intuition and expression in §9 of the First Logical Investigation, he has rendered Husserl's German "eventuell" as "éventuellement." The French translators of the *Logische Untersuchungen* have translated it in the same way. Findlay renders the term as "possibly." I am rendering it, however, as "contingently," since both the German and the French terms have the sense of "as it may well turn out" or "as it may well happen." But one can see that both the German and French terms contain the word "event." What seems to come about *contingently* happens as an *event.* Moreover, it happens eventually in the sense of a possibility that was already there.

22. I have rendered Derrida's neologism "différance," which has a double meaning of defer and differ, by the same term. As we see at the beginning of chapter 7 and in its closing section, the French verb "différer" means both to defer and to differ. For more on this term, see Derrida's essay "Différance," which is collected in *Margins of Philosophy,* 1–28.

23. I have rendered the French term "écart" as "hiatus." This term appears frequently throughout French thought of the 1960s.

24. Since *Voice and Phenomenon* is a book in ontology (the question of the meaning of being as presence), it was necessary to be particularly attentive to Derrida's use of ontological terms. These terms are frequently compounds such as "être-indice" (20 of the French); "être-pour" (24, 85 of the French); "être-signe" (25 of the French); "être-devant" (83, 84, 111 of the French); "être-idéal" (84 of the French); "être-originaire" (95 of the French); and "être-mort" (108 of the French). These hyphenated terms have been respectively rendered as "indication-being"; "being-for"; "sign-being"; "being-in-front"; "ideal-being"; "originary-being"; and "being-dead."

25. The French word "scène" appears as early as the introduction (8, there rendered as "scene," and 14, as "stage"), but it plays almost a thematic role in both chapters 6 and 7. It has usually been rendered as "scene" in order to be consistent with Derrida's contemporaneous essay on Freud called, in English, "Freud and the Scene of Writing" ("Freud et la scène de l'écriture"); this essay is collected in *Writing and Difference*, 196–231. The French word "scène," however, also means "stage" (and by metonymy "theater"), which implies the idea of representation, of a spectacle with several acts and of something watched or looked at.

VOICE AND PHENOMENON

If we read the word "I" without knowing who wrote it, it is perhaps not meaningless, but it is at least foreign to its normal signification.

—Husserl, *Logical Investigations*

A name uttered in front of us makes us think of the Dresden Gallery and of our last visit there: we wander through the rooms and stop before a picture by Teniers which represents a picture gallery. Let us suppose, moreover, that the pictures in this gallery represent again pictures which for their part would make visible inscriptions that we are able to decipher, etc.

—Husserl, *Ideas I*

I have spoken both of "sound" and "voice." I mean to say that the sound was one of distinct, of even wonderfully, thrillingly distinct, syllabification. M. Valdemar *spoke*, obviously in reply to the question. . . . He now said:

"Yes;—no;—*I have been sleeping*—and now—now—*I am dead.*"

—Edgar Allan Poe, "The Facts in the Case of M. Valdemar"

Introduction

<1>The *Logical Investigations* (1900–1901) opened a path down which, as is well known, all of phenomenology has been pushed. Until the fourth edition (1928), there was no fundamental shift; nothing was put back into question in a decisive way. Some things were of course rearranged, and there was a powerful work of explanation. *Ideas I* and *Formal and Transcendental Logic* unfold, without a break, the concepts of intentional or noematic sense, the difference between the two strata of analytics in the broad sense (pure morphology of judgments and consequence-logic), and they remove the deductivist or nomological restriction that has until now affected the concept of science in general.*,1 The conceptual premises of the *Logical Investigations* are still at work in *The Crisis* and the texts associated with it, in particular in "The Origin of Geometry,"[2] notably when they concern all the problems of signification and of language in general. In this domain more than anywhere else, a patient reading would bring to light in the *Logical Investigations* the germinal structure of all of Husserl's thought. On each page the necessity—or the implicit practice—of the eidetic and phenomenological reductions can be read, the detectable presence of all of that to which the reductions give access.

Now the First Logical Investigation ("Ausdruck und Bedeutung")†,3 <2> opens with a chapter devoted to the "essential distinctions" that rigorously order all the later analyses. And the coherence of this chapter owes everything to a distinction that is proposed in the first paragraph: the word "sign" (*Zeichen*) would have a "double sense" (*ein Doppelsinn*).[4] The sign "sign" can mean "expression" (*Ausdruck*) or "indication" (*Anzeichen*).[5]

---

* Edmund Husserl, *Formal and Transcendental Logic*, §35b, pp. 103–4.
† With the exception of some openings and indispensable anticipations, the present essay analyzes the doctrine of meaning such that it is constituted in the First Logical Investigation. In order to follow better its difficult and tortuous itinerary, we have generally abstained from comparisons, similarities, or oppositions which here and there seem to confront us between the Husserlian theory of meaning and other classical or modern theories of meaning. Each time that we go beyond the text of the First Logical Investigation, we are doing this in order to indicate the principle of a general interpretation of Husserl's thought and in order to sketch a systematic reading that we hope to attempt one day.

From what question shall we receive and read this distinction, whose stakes appear to be quite high?

Before proposing this purely "phenomenological" distinction between the two senses of the word "sign" or rather before recognizing the distinction, before raising it up into what intends to be a simple description, Husserl proceeds to a sort of implicit phenomenological reduction. He puts out of play all constituted knowledge. He insists on the necessary absence of presuppositions (*Voraussetzungslosigkeit*), whether they come from metaphysics, from psychology, or from the natural sciences. The starting point in the "Faktum" of language is not a presupposition as long as we are attentive to the contingency of the example. The analyses thus carried out keep their "sense" and their "epistemological value"—their value in the order of the theory of knowledge (*erkenntnistheoretischen Wert*)—whether languages exist or not, whether beings such as humans actually make use of languages or not, whether humans or a nature exist really or merely "in the imagination and on the basis of the mode of possibility."[6]

The most general form of our question is thus prescribed. Do not the phenomenological necessity, the rigor and the subtlety of <3> Husserl's analysis, the demands to which it responds and the demands we must first of all satisfy, nevertheless dissimulate a metaphysical presupposition? Do they not hide a dogmatic or speculative attachment which would, certainly, not restrain the phenomenological critique from outside of itself, which would not be the residue of an unnoticed naïveté, but would *constitute* phenomenology from its inside, in its critical project and in the instituting value of its own premises? It would be restrained precisely in what phenomenology will recognize soon as the source and the guarantee of all value, "the principle of all principles," namely, the originary giving evidentness, the *present* or the *presence* of sense in a full and originary intuition. In other words, we are not wondering whether some sort of metaphysical heritage has been able, here or there, to limit the vigilance of a phenomenologist. Rather we are wondering whether the *phenomenological* form of this vigilance is not already ordered by metaphysics itself. In the lines that we just evoked, the mistrust in regard to the metaphysical presuppositions is given already as the condition of an authentic "theory of knowledge," as if this project of a theory of knowledge, even when it has become independent from some such speculative system by means of a "critique," does not belong, from the moment it starts up, to the history of metaphysics. Isn't it the case that the idea of knowledge and a theory of knowledge are metaphysical in themselves?

Therefore what would be at issue, on the basis of the privileged example of the sign, will be to see the phenomenological critique of metaphysics announce itself as a moment within the security that metaphysics provides. Better, what would be at issue will be to begin to verify that the resource of the phenomenological critique is the metaphysical project itself, in its historical completion and in the purity of its origin albeit restored.

We have attempted elsewhere to follow the movement by means <4> of which Husserl, by constantly criticizing metaphysical speculation, was truly aiming his critique only at the perversion or the degeneration of what he continues to think and to want to restore as authentic metaphysics or *philosophia prote̅.**,7 Concluding his *Cartesian Meditations,* Husserl still opposes authentic metaphysics (the one that will owe its achievement to phenomenology) to metaphysics in the usual sense. The results that he presents then are, he writes,

> metaphysical, if it is true that ultimate knowledge of being should be called metaphysical. On the other hand, what we have here is anything but metaphysical in the usual sense: a historically degenerate metaphysics which by no means conforms to the spirit in which metaphysics as "first philosophy" was originally instituted. Phenomenology's purely intuitive, concrete, and also apodictic mode of demonstration excludes all "metaphysical adventure," all speculative excess.[8]

One would be able to bring to light the single and permanent motive for all the mistakes and all the perversions that Husserl denounces in "degenerate" metaphysics, across a multiplicity of domains, themes, and arguments: it is always a blindness in the face of the authentic mode of *ideality,* of that which *is,* which can be *repeated* indefinitely in the *identity* of its *presence* because of the very fact that it *does not exist,* is not *reell,* is *ir-reell,* not in the sense of fiction, but in another sense which will be able to receive several names, whose possibility will allow us to speak of the non-reality and of the necessity of essence, of the noema, of the intelligible object and of non-mundanity in general.[9] This non-mundanity, not being another mundanity, this ideality not being an existent that comes down from the sky, will always have its origin in the possibility of the repetition of the act that produces it. So that the possibility of this repetition can be open *idealiter* to infinity, it is necessary that one ideal form secures this unity of the *indefinitely* and the *idealiter:* this is the present, or rather the presence of the *living present.* The ultimate form of ideality, the one in which in the last analysis we can anticipate or recall all <5> repetition, the

---

* Jacques Derrida, "La phénoménologie et la clôture de la métaphysique," in *ΕΠΟΧΕΣ,* Athens, February 1966.

ideality of ideality is the *living present*, the self-presence of transcendental life. Presence has always been and will always be, to infinity, the form in which—we can say this apodictically—the infinite diversity of contents will be produced. The opposition—the inaugural opposition of meta-physics—between form and matter, finds in the concrete ideality of the living present its ultimate and radical justification. We shall come upon the enigma of the concept of *life* in the expressions "the living present" and "transcendental life" again. Let us note, however, in order to specify our intention here, that phenomenology appears to us to be tormented if not contested, from the inside, by means of its own descriptions of the movement of temporalization and of the constitution of intersubjectivity. At the greatest depth of what connects these two decisive moments of the description together, one sees an irreducible non-presence recognized as a constituting value, and with it a non-life or a non-presence of the living present, a non-belonging of the living present to itself, a non-originarity that cannot be eradicated. The names that it receives only make its resis-tance to the form of presence more vivid; *in two words*, what is at issue is: (1) the necessary passage from retention to *re-presentation* (*Vergegenwär-tigung*) in the constitution of the presence of a temporal object (*Gegen-stand*) whose identity can be repeated; (2) the necessary passage through *appresentation* in the relation to the *alter ego*, that is, in the relation to what also makes possible an ideal objectivity in general, intersubjectivity being the condition of objectivity and this objectivity being absolute only in the case of ideal objects. In the two cases, what is named as a modification of presentation (*re*-presentation and *ap*-presentation) (*Vergegenwärtigung* or *Appräsentation*) does not supervene upon presentation, but conditions it by fissuring it *a priori*. That does not call into question the apodictic-ity of the phenomenological-transcendental description. It does not cut into the founding value of presence. This expression, moreover, "the founding value of presence," is a pleonastic expression. What is at issue, however, is to make the original and non-empirical space of <6> non-foundation appear, as the irreducible emptiness from which the security of presence in the metaphysical form of ideality is decided and from which this security removes itself. It is within this horizon that we are here interrogating the phenomenological concept of the sign.

The concept of metaphysics with which we are working will have to be determined, and the generality of this question, which is too large, must be narrowed here. In the case in point, we are narrowing down the question to this: how to justify first of all the *decision* which subordinates a reflection on the sign to a logic? And if the concept of sign precedes logical reflection, is given to logic, is delivered to its critique, from where does the concept of the sign come? Where does the essence of the sign, in relation to which this concept is regulated, come from? What grants authority to a theory of knowledge in order to determine the essence and origin of language? Such a *decision,* we do not attribute it to Husserl; he takes it up explicitly, or rather, he takes up explicitly its heritage and validity. The consequences of this are limitless. On the one hand, Husserl has had to defer, from one end of his itinerary to another, every explicit meditation on the essence of language *in general.* He puts the meditation on the essence of language in general "out of play" in *Formal and Transcendental Logic.*[10] And, as Fink has indeed shown, Husserl never posed the question of the transcendental *logos,* of the inherited language in which phenomenology produces and exhibits the results of the workings of the reduction. The unity between ordinary language (or the language of traditional metaphysics) and the language of phenomenology is never broken despite all the precautions, quotation marks, renovations and innovations. The transformation of a traditional concept into an indicative or metaphorical concept does not absolve the heritage; it imposes questions which Husserl has never attempted to answer. This is due to the fact that, on the other hand, by being interested in language only within the horizon of rationality, by determining the *logos* on the basis of logic, Husserl has in fact, and in a traditional way, determined the essence of language by starting from logicity as the normalcy of its *telos.* What we would like to suggest here is that this *telos* <7> is the *telos* of being as presence.

Thus, for example, when what is at issue is the redefinition of the relation between pure grammar and pure logic (a relation that traditional logic would have missed, since it was perverted by metaphysical presuppositions), when what is at issue therefore is the constitution of a pure morphology of *Bedeutungen* (we are not translating this word for reasons that will appear in a moment), the re-apprehension of pure grammaticality, the system of rules that allow us to recognize whether a discourse in general is really a discourse—if it makes *sense* or if falsehood or the absurdity of contradiction (*Widersinnigkeit*) do not make it incomprehensible and do not deprive it of the quality of meaningful discourse, do not render it *sinnlos*—then the pure generality of this meta-empirical grammar does not cover the whole field of the possibility of language in general; it does not exhaust the whole extent of the *a priori* of language. The pure generality of the meta-empirical grammar concerns only the *logical a priori* of language; it is *pure logical grammar.* This restriction is functioning from the beginning, although Husserl did not stress it in the first edition of the *Logical Investigations:*

> In the First Edition, I spoke of "pure grammar," a name conceived and explicitly devised as being analogous to Kant's "pure science of nature."

But to the extent that it cannot, however, be asserted that the pure
morphology of *Bedeutungen* takes in the entire grammatical *a priori* in its
universality—since for example the communicative relations between
psychical subjects, so important for the grammar, involve their own
a priori, the expression "pure logical grammar" is preferable.[11]

Carving out the logical *a priori* within the general *a priori* of language does not extract a region. As we are going to see, it designates the
dignity of a *telos,* the purity of a norm, and the essence of a destination.
<8> By locating in the First Logical Investigation the roots that Husserl's
later discourse will never disturb, we would like to show here therefore
that the movement in which the whole of phenomenology is already engaged repeats the original intention of metaphysics itself. The value of
presence (in the two connected senses of the proximity of what is set out
as an object of an intuition and the proximity of the temporal present
which gives its form to the clear and actual intuition of the object), the
last court of appeal for this whole discourse, modifies itself, without its
being lost, every time what is at issue is the presence of any object what-
soever to consciousness in the clear evidence of a fulfilled intuition or
when what is at issue is self-presence in consciousness—"consciousness"
meaning nothing other than the possibility of the self-presence of the
present in the living present.[12] Each time that this value of presence is
threatened, Husserl will awaken it, will recall it, will make it return to
itself in the form of the *telos,* that is, in the form of the Idea in the Kantian sense. There is no *ideality* unless an Idea in the Kantian sense is at
work, opening the possibility of an indefinite, the infinity of a prescribed
progress, or the infinity of permitted repetitions. This ideality is the very
form in which the presence of an object in general can be indefinitely
repeated as the *same.* The non-reality of the *Bedeutung,* the non-reality of
the ideal object, the non-reality of the inclusion of the sense or of the
noema in consciousness (Husserl will say that the noema does not belong
in a reell manner—*reell*—to consciousness) will provide therefore the
security that the presence to consciousness will be able to be repeated
indefinitely: ideal presence to an ideal or transcendental consciousness.
Ideality is the salvation or the mastery of presence in repetition. In its
purity, this presence is the presence of nothing that *exists* in the world;
it is in correlation with acts of repetition which are themselves ideal. Is
this to say that what opens the repetition to infinity or what is opened
in repetition when the movement of idealization is secured *is* a certain
relation of an "existent" to his death? Is this to say that "transcendental
life" is the scene <9> of this relation? It is too early to say that. First, it
is necessary to pass through the problem of language. We shall not be

surprised to discover that language is really the medium of this play of presence and absence. Is it not in language, is not language first of all the very thing in which *life* and *ideality* could seem to be united? Now, we must consider *on the one hand* that the element of signification—or the substance of expression—which seems best to preserve at once ideality and living presence in all of its forms, is living speech, the spirituality of the breath as *phonē*. On the other hand, we must consider that phenomenology, the metaphysics of presence in the form of ideality, is also a philosophy of *life*.

It is a philosophy of life not only because, in its center, death is recognized as having nothing but an empirical and extrinsic signification, the signification of mundane accident, but also because the source of sense in general is always determined as the act of a thing that *lives*, as the act of a living being, as *Lebendigkeit*. Now the unity of living, the hearth fire of the *Lebendigkeit* which diffracts its light into all the fundamental concepts of phenomenology (*Leben, Erlebnis, lebendige Gegenwart, Geistigkeit*, etc.), escapes the transcendental reduction, and as the unity of mundane life and transcendental life, blazes open even the passage for the reduction.[13] When empirical life or even the pure region of the psychical are bracketed, what Husserl discovers is still a transcendental *life* or in the last analysis the transcendentality of a *living* present—and Husserl thematizes it without so much as posing the question of this unity of the concept of *life*. "Consciousness without a soul" (*seelenloses*), whose essential possibility is presented in *Ideas I* (§54), is still a *living* transcendental consciousness. If we conclude, with a gesture that is in fact very Husserlian in its style, that the concepts of empirical life (or in general mundane life) and transcendental life are radically heterogeneous and that a purely indicative or metaphorical relation is going on between the two names, then the possibility of this <10> relation bears the entire weight of the question. The common root that makes all of these metaphors possible appears to us to still be the concept of *life*. In the last analysis, between the pure psychical—a region of the world that is opposed to transcendental consciousness and is discovered by means of the reduction of the totality of the natural, transcendent world—and the pure transcendental life, there is, Husserl says, a relation of *parallelism*.

Phenomenological psychology will in fact have to remind any working psychology of its background of eidetic presuppositions and the conditions of its own language. It will be incumbent on phenomenological psychology to settle the sense of the concepts of psychology, and first of all the sense of what we call the *psychē*. But what is going to allow us to distinguish this phenomenological psychology, which is an eidetic and *a priori*, descriptive science, from transcendental phenomenology itself?

What is going to allow us to distinguish the epochē which discovers the immanent domain of the purely psychical from the transcendental epochē itself? For the field opened by this pure psychology has a privilege in regard to the other regions, and its generality dominates all other regions. All lived-experiences arise from it necessarily and the sense of every region or of every determinate object is announced by way of this pure psychology. Thus too the dependence of the purely psychical in regard to transcendental consciousness, which is the archi-region, is absolutely singular. The domain of pure psychological experience in fact coincides with the totality of the domain of what Husserl calls transcendental experience. And yet, despite this perfect *coincidence,* a radical difference remains, which has nothing in common with any other difference. This is a difference which in fact distinguishes nothing, a difference which separates no being, no lived-experience, no determinate signification. This is a difference however which, without altering anything, changes all the signs, and it is a difference in which alone the possibility of a transcendental question holds, that is, the possibility of freedom itself. This is, therefore, the fundamental difference without which no other difference in the world would make sense or even have a chance of appearing *as such.* Without the possibility and without the <11> recognition of such a *doubling* (*Verdoppelung*), whose rigor will tolerate no duplicity, without this invisible distance stretched between the two acts of the epochē, transcendental phenomenology would be destroyed at its root. The difficulty is based on the fact that this doubling of sense must not correspond to any ontological double. For example, and briefly put, my transcendental I[14] is radically different, Husserl explicitly states, from my natural and human I.[15] And yet, the transcendental I is distinguished from the natural and human I by nothing, by nothing that might be determined by the natural sense of distinction. The (transcendental) I is not an other. It is especially not the metaphysical or formal phantom of the empirical self.[16] This is what would lead to denouncing the idea that the absolute spectator I is the theoretical image and metaphor of its literal psychical self; as well this means denouncing every analogical language of which we must at times make use in order to announce the transcendental reduction and in order to describe this unheard-of "object" which is the psychical self over against the absolute transcendental ego. Truly, no language is equal to this operation by which the transcendental ego constitutes and opposes its own mundane self, that is, opposes its soul, by reflecting itself in a *verweltlichende Selbstapperzeption.*[*,17] The pure soul is this strange self-

* Husserl, *Cartesian Meditations,* §45.

objectivation (*Selbstobjektivierung*) of the monad by and in itself.*,[18] There also the Soul proceeds from the One (the monadic ego) and can freely turn itself back toward the monadic ego in a Reduction.

All of these difficulties are concentrated in the enigmatic concept of "parallelism." Husserl evokes the astonishing, admirable "parallel nature" and even "the coincidence, if we may put it this way," of phenomenological psychology and transcendental phenomenology, "both understood as eidetic disciplines."† "The one <12> inhabits the other, so to speak, implicitly." This *nothing* that distinguishes the parallels, this nothing without which no explication, that is, no language, would be able to develop freely in the truth without being distorted by some real milieu, this nothing without which no transcendental, that is, philosophical, question would be able to take a breath, this nothing arises, if we can say this, when the *totality* of the world is neutralized in its existence and reduced to its phenomenon. *This operation is that of the transcendental reduction; in any case, it cannot be that of the psycho-phenomenological reduction.* The pure eidetics of psychical lived-experience concerns, undoubtedly, no determinate existence, no empirical factuality; it calls for no signification that is transcendent to consciousness. But the essences that it settles *intrinsically* presuppose the existence of the world in that kind of mundane region called the *psychē*. Moreover, we must notice that this parallelism does more than release the transcendental ether. What it does is make more mysterious still (and it alone is capable of doing this) the sense of the *psychical* and of psychical *life,* that is, it makes more mysterious the sense of a *mundanity* that is capable of bearing and in some way nurturing *transcendentality,* having a domain equal in extent to transcendentality without, however, merging with the transcendental in some total *adequation.* To conclude from this *parallelism* with an *adequation* is the most tempting, the most subtle but also the most obscuring of confusions: *transcendental psychologism.* Against this, it is necessary to maintain the precarious and threatened distance between the parallels; against transcendental psychologism it is necessary to question constantly. Now, since transcendental consciousness is not impaired in its sense by the hypothesis of a destruction of the world (*Ideas I,* §49), "it is certain that we can think a consciousness without a body and, as paradoxical as it may seem, without a soul [*seelenloses*]."[19] And yet, transcendental consciousness *is nothing more or other* than psychological consciousness. Transcendental <13> psychologism does not understand that. It does not understand

---

* Husserl, *Cartesian Meditations,* §57.
† Husserl, *Phänomenologishe Psychologie,* p. 343.

that if the world needs a *supplement of soul,* the soul, which is in the world, needs this *supplementary nothing* that is the transcendental and without which no world would appear. If we are attentive to Husserl's renewal of the notion of the "transcendental," then we must do the opposite of transcendental psychologism and guard against endowing this distance with some sort of reality. We must not substantialize this inconsistency or turn it into, perhaps by simple analogy, some thing or some factor of the world. This would be to freeze the light at its source. If language never escapes from analogy, even if it is analogy through and through, it must, having reached this point, and at this very point, freely take up its own destruction and cast metaphors against metaphors. This is to obey the most traditional of imperatives, an imperative that has received its most explicit (but not the most original) form in the *Enneads,* an imperative that has never stopped being faithfully transmitted all the way down to the *Introduction to Metaphysics* (especially that of Bergson). This war of language against itself is the price that we have to pay in order to think sense and the question of the origin of sense. We see that this war is not one war among many. As a polemic for the possibility of sense and of the world, this war takes place in this *difference,* which, as we have seen, cannot inhabit the world, but only language, in its transcendental restlessness. In truth, far from merely inhabiting language, this difference is also its origin and its abode. Language keeps watch over the difference that keeps watch over language.

Later, in his *Nachwort zu meinen Ideen* (1930) and in the *Cartesian Meditations* (§14 and 57), Husserl will evoke again, and briefly, this "precise parallelism" between "the pure psychology of consciousness" and "the transcendental phenomenology of consciousness."[20] And he will then say, in order to impugn transcendental psychologism which "makes an authentic philosophy impossible" (*Cartesian Meditations,* §14), we have to practice at all costs the "Nuancierung" which distinguishes the parallels, one of which is in the world and the other is outside of the world without being in another world, that is, without stopping <14> to be, *like every parallel, alongside* and *right next to the other.*[21] At all costs, it is necessary to collect and shelter in our discourse these subtle (*geringfügigen*), frivolous, "seemingly trivial nuances" that "decisively decide the paths and the detours [*Wege und Abwege*] of philosophy" (*Cartesian Meditations,* §14). Our discourse must shelter these nuances within itself and at once thereby *in them re-secure its possibility and its rigor.* But the strange unity of these two parallels, what relates the one to the other, does not let itself be distributed by the parallels, and by dividing itself finally welds the transcendental to its other: this strange unity is *life.* One sees in fact very quickly that the sole kernel of the concept of *psychē* is life as self-relation, whether the relation is produced or not in the form of consciousness. "Living" is therefore the name of what precedes the reduction and escapes finally from all the distributions that the reduction brings to light. Life, however, is its own distribution and its own opposition to its other. By determining "living" in this way, we just therefore named the resource of the insecurity of discourse, the point at which precisely it can no longer *re-secure its possibility and its rigor in the nuance.* This concept of life is then grasped in an agency which is no longer that of pre-transcendental naïveté, in the language of everyday life or in the language of biological science. But if this ultra-transcendental concept of life allows us to think life (in the everyday sense or in the sense of biology) and if it has never been inscribed in any language, this concept of life perhaps calls for *another name.*

We will be less astonished confronting the effort of phenomenology—an effort that is laborious and oblique, even tenacious—to keep watch over speech, in order to assert an essential link between the *logos* and the *phonē,* since the privilege of consciousness (about which Husserl fundamentally never wondered *what consciousness is,* despite all the admirable, interminable and in many regards revolutionary meditations that he devoted to it) is only the possibility of the living voice. Since self-consciousness appears only in its relation to an object whose presence it can keep watch over and repeat, self-consciousness is never perfectly foreign or prior to the possibility of language. As we shall see, Husserl <15> doubtlessly wanted to maintain an originarily silent, "pre-expressive" layer of lived-experience. But since the possibility of constituting ideal objects belongs to the essence of consciousness, and since these ideal objects are historical products, which appear only thanks to acts of creation or of intention, the element of consciousness and the element of language will be more and more difficult to discern. Now, is it not the case that their indiscernability will introduce non-presence and difference (mediacy, the sign, referral, etc.) right into the heart of self-presence? This difficulty *calls for* a response. This response is called the voice. The enigma of the voice is rich and profound because of all the things to which it seems to be responding. That the voice simulates the "keeping watch" over presence and that the history of spoken language is the archive of this simulation from now on prevents us from considering the "difficulty" to which the voice responds, in Husserl's phenomenology, either as a systematic difficulty or as a contradiction that would be specific to his phenomenology. That as well prevents us from describing this simulation, whose structure involves an infinite complexity, as an illusion, a phantasm, or a hallucination. These last concepts in fact refer to the simulation of language as to their common root.

This "difficulty" structures Husserl's whole discourse, and we must recognize the work it does. By exploiting all of its resources with the greatest critical refinement, Husserl will radicalize the necessary privilege of the *phonē* which is implied by the entire history of metaphysics. For Husserl will not recognize an originative affinity with the *logos* in general in the sonorous substance or in the physical voice, or in the body of the voice in the world; rather the originative affinity will be recognized in the phenomenological voice, in the voice in its transcendental flesh, in the breath, in intentional animation which transforms the body of the word into flesh, which turns the *Körper* into *Leib*, a *geistige Leiblichkeit.* The phenomenological voice would be this spiritual flesh which continues to speak and to be present to itself—*to hear itself*—in the absence of the <16> world. Of course, what we grant to the voice is granted to the language of *words,* to a language constituted from unities—which we could believe irreducible and indecomposable—welding the signified concept onto the signifying "phonic complex." Despite the vigilance of the description, a perhaps naive treatment of the concept of "word" has no doubt failed to resolve in phenomenology the tension between its two major motives: the purity of formalism and the radicality of intuitionism.

That the privilege of presence as consciousness can be *established*—that is, can be constituted historically as well as demonstrated—only by means of the excellence of the voice is a claim whose obviousness has never held center stage in phenomenology. According to a mode that is neither simply operative nor directly thematic, in a place that is neither central nor lateral, the necessity of this claim's obviousness seems to have secured a sort of "grip" on all phenomenology.[22] The nature of this "grip" is badly conceived in the concepts usually devoted to the philosophy of the history of philosophy. But our purpose here is not to meditate directly on the form of this "grip." Our purpose is merely to show it as already at work—and powerfully—from the very beginning of the First Logical Investigation.

1

Sign and Signs

<17> Husserl begins by pointing out a confusion. Within the word "sign" (*Zeichen*), always in ordinary language and at times in philosophical language, are hidden two heterogeneous concepts: that of *expression* (*Ausdruck*), which we often mistakenly hold as being the synonym of the sign in general, and that of *indication* (*Anzeichen*). Now, according to Husserl, there are some signs that express nothing because these signs carry—we must still say this in German—nothing that we can call *Bedeutung* or *Sinn*. This is what indication is. Certainly, indication is a sign, like expression. But it is different from expression because it is, insofar as it is an indication, deprived of *Bedeutung* or *Sinn: bedeutunglos, sinnlos*. Nevertheless it is not a sign without signification. Essentially, there cannot be a sign without signification, a signifier without a signified. This is why the traditional translation of *Bedeutung* by "signification," although it is established and nearly inevitable, risks blurring Husserl's entire text, rendering it unintelligible in its axial intention, and consequently rendering unintelligible all of what will depend on these first "essential distinctions." One can say with Husserl in German, without absurdity, that a sign (*Zeichen*) is deprived of *Bedeutung* (is *bedeutungslos*, is not *bedeutsam*), but one cannot say in French, without contradiction, that *un signe* is deprived of *signification*.[1] In German one can speak of expression (*Ausdruck*) as a *bedeutsame Zeichen*, which Husserl does. One cannot, without redundancy, <18> translate *bedeutsame Zeichen* into French as *signe signifiant*, which lets us imagine, against the evidence and against Husserl's intention, that we could have *des signes non signifiants*. While being suspicious of the established French translations, we must nevertheless confess that it will always be difficult to replace them. This is why our remarks are nothing less than criticisms aimed at the existing, valuable translations. We shall try nevertheless to propose some solutions which will keep to being halfway between commentary and translation. They will thus be valid only within the limits of Husserl's texts. Most often, when we are confronting a difficulty, we shall, according to a procedure whose value is at times contestable, retain the German word while attempting to clarify it by means of the analysis.

In this way, it will be very quickly confirmed that, for Husserl, the expressivity of the expression—which always assumes the ideality of a

Bedeutung—has an irreducible link to the possibility of spoken discourse (*Rede*). Expression is a purely linguistic sign and, in the first analysis, this is precisely what distinguishes it from indication. Although spoken discourse is a very complex structure, involving always, *in fact*, an indicative layer which, as we shall see, we shall have the greatest trouble trying to hold within its limits, Husserl reserves for it the exclusivity of the right to expression and therefore the exclusivity of pure logicity.[2] Without violating Husserl's intention, one could define, if not translate, "bedeuten" by "vouloir-dire" at once in the sense of a speaking subject that *wants to say*, "expressing himself," as Husserl says, "about something"—and in the sense of an expression that *means*.[*,3] We can then be assured that the *Bedeutung* is always *what* someone or a discourse *means* <*veulent dire*>: always a sense of discourse, a discursive content.

In contrast to Frege, Husserl, as we know, does not distinguish, in the *Logical Investigations*, between *Sinn* and *Bedeutung*:

> Besides, for us, <19> *Bedeutung* means the same thing as *Sinn* [*gilt als gleichbedeutend mit Sinn*]. On the one hand, it is very convenient, especially in the case of this concept, to have at one's disposal parallel, interchangeable terms, particularly since the sense of the term *Bedeutung* is itself to be investigated. A further consideration is our ingrained habit to use the two words as meaning the same thing. In these conditions, it seems a rather dubious step if their *Bedeutungen* are differentiated, and if (as G. Frege has proposed) we use one for *Bedeutung* in our sense, and the other for the objects expressed.[4]

In *Ideas I*, the dissociation that intervenes between the two terms does not at all have the same function as in Frege, and it confirms our reading: *Bedeutung* is reserved for the ideal sense content of *verbal* expression, of spoken discourse, while sense (*Sinn*) covers the whole noematic sphere, including its non-expressive stratum:

> We begin with the familiar distinction between the sensuous, so to speak, corporeal side of expression, and its non-sensuous or "spiritual" side. We need not enter into a closer examination of the first side; likewise, we need not consider the manner of unifying both sides. Obviously, they too designate headings for not unimportant phenomenological problems. We shall restrict our regard exclusively to "signifying"

---

* "To mean," "meaning" <in English> are good equivalents for "bedeuten," "Bedeutung," which we do not have in French.

[*bedeuten*] and "Bedeutung." Originally, these words concerned only the
linguistic sphere [*sprachliche Sphäre*], that of "expressing" [*des Ausdrück-
ens*]. But one can scarcely avoid and, at the same time, take an important cognitive step, extending the *Bedeutung* of these words and suitably
modifying them so that they can find application of a certain kind to
the whole noetico-noematic sphere: thus application to all acts, be
they now interwoven [*verflochten*] with expressive acts or not. Thus we
have continued to speak of "sense" [*Sinn*] in the case of all intentional
lived-experience—a word which is used in general as an equivalent
<20> to *Bedeutung*. For the sake of distinctness we shall prefer the term
Bedeutung for the old concept, and, in particular, in the complex locu-
tion of "logical *Bedeutung*" or "expressive *Bedeutung*." We shall continue
to use the word "sense" as before in the most all-inclusive range.[5]

After having asserted, in a passage to which we shall have to return, that
there exists a pre-expressive stratum of lived-experience or sense, and
then that this stratum of sense could always receive expression and *Bedeutung*, Husserl proposes that "logical *Bedeutung* is an expression."[6]

The difference between indication and expression appears very
quickly, over the course of the description, as a difference that is more
functional than *substantial*. Indication and expression are functions or
signifying relations and not terms. One and the same phenomenon can
be apprehended as expression or as indication, as a discursive sign or as
a non-discursive sign. That depends on the intentional lived-experience
that animates it. The functional character of the description immediately
shows the extent of the difficulty and gets us right to its center. Two functions can be interwoven or entangled in the same concatenation of signs,
in the same signification. Husserl speaks first of the addition or of the
juxtaposition of one function with the other: ". . . signs in the sense of
indication [*Anzeichen*] (notes, marks, etc.) *do not express,* unless they fulfill,
in addition to [Husserl's emphasis, *neben,* "besides"] the indicative function, a function of *Bedeutung*."[7] But a few lines later, he will speak of intimate intrication, of entanglement (*Verflechtung*). This word will reappear
often, at decisive moments, and this will not be by chance. It appears already in the first section: "Meaning [*bedeuten* <*vouloir-dire*>]—in communicative discourse [*in mitteilender Rede*]—is always interwoven [*verflochten*]
in a relation with this indication-being."[8]

We therefore already know that, *in fact,* the discursive sign and consequently the meaning <*le vouloir-dire*> is *always* entangled, *gripped* within
an indicative system. <21> The expressive and logical purity of the *Bedeutung* that Husserl wants to grasp as the possibility of the *Logos* is gripped,
that is, contaminated—*in fact and always* (*allzeit verflochten ist*) insofar as

the *Bedeutung* is gripped within a communicative discourse. Of course, as we shall see, communication itself is for Husserl a stratum that is extrinsic to expression. But each time that an expression is produced in fact, it carries a communicative value, even if the expression does not exhaust itself in communication or if this value is simply associated with it.

It will be necessary to specify the modalities of this interweaving. But it is clear from now on that this factual necessity of entanglement which intimately associates expression and indication must not, in Husserl's eyes, undermine the possibility of a rigorous essential distinction. This possibility is purely juridical and phenomenological. The whole analysis will move forward therefore in this hiatus between fact and right, existence and essence, reality and the intentional function. By indeed leaping over the mediations and by reversing the apparent order, we would be tempted to say that this hiatus, which defines the very space of phenomenology, does not preexist the question of language, and it is not inserted into phenomenology as within one domain or as one problem among others. It is opened up, on the contrary, only in and by the possibility of language. And its juridical value, the right to a distinction between fact and intentional right, depends entirely on language and, in language, on the validity of a radical distinction between indication and expression.

Let us pursue our reading. Every expression would therefore be gripped, despite itself, by an indicative process. But the opposite, Husserl recognizes, is not true. We might therefore be tempted to turn the expressive sign into a species of the genus "indication." In this case, we would have to say in the end that speech, whatever the dignity or whatever the originality we still grant it, is only a form of gesture. In its essential center and not only by means of what Husserl considers as its accidents (its physical side, its communicative function), <22> speech belongs, without exceeding it, to the general system of signification. This system would be merged with the system of indication.

This is precisely what Husserl contests. In order to do that, he must therefore demonstrate that expression is not a species of indication even though all expressions are mixed with indication, the reverse not being true. Husserl writes,

> If one limits oneself to expressions employed in living colloquy, as one usually does involuntarily when expression is in question, the concept of an indication seems to apply more widely than that of an expression, but this does not mean that its content is the genus of which an expression is the species. *To mean [bedeuten <vouloir-dire>] is not a particular species of sign-being [Zeichenseins] in the sense of indication [Anzeige]. It has a*

narrower application only because meaning [*bedeuten*]—in communicative discourse—is always entangled [*verflochten*] with indication-being
[*Anzeichensein*], and this in its turn leads to a wider concept, since meaning is also capable of occurring outside of this entanglement.*.9

In order to demonstrate the rupture of the species-genus relation,
we then have to rediscover, if there is any, a phenomenological situation in which expression is no longer tied up in this entanglement, is
no longer interwoven with indication. Since this contamination is always
produced in real colloquy (at once because in real colloquy expression
indicates a content that is forever hidden from intuition, namely, the
lived-experience of the other, and because the ideal content of the *Bedeutung* and the spiritual side of the expression are united in real colloquy with the sensible side), it is in a language without communication,
in a monological discourse, in the absolutely lowest register of the voice
of the "*solitary life of the soul*" (*in einem Seelenleben*) that it is necessary to
track down the unmarred purity of expression. Through a strange paradox, the meaning <*le vouloir-dire*> would isolate the concentrated purity
of ex-pressivity only when the relation to a certain *outside* would be suspended. Only to a certain outside, because this <23> reduction will not
erase and indeed shall reveal in pure expressivity the relation to the object, the aim of an objective ideality, over and against the intention of
meaning <*vouloir-dire*>, over and against the *Bedeutungsintention*. What
we just called a paradox is in truth only the phenomenological project
in its essence. Beyond the opposition between "idealism" and "realism,"
"subjectivism" and "objectivism," etc., phenomenological transcendental
idealism responds to the necessity to describe the *ob*jectivity of the *ob*ject
(*Gegenstand*) and the *pre*sence of the present (*Gegenwart*)—and the objectivity in presence—on the basis of an "interiority" or rather on the basis
of a self-proximity, of an *ownness* (*Eigenheit*) which is not a simple *inside*,
but the intimate possibility of the relation to an over-there and to an
outside in general. This is why the essence of intentional consciousness
will be revealed (for example in *Ideas I*, §49) only in the reduction of the
totality of the existing world in general.

This movement is already sketched in the First Logical Investigation in relation to expression and meaning <*vouloir-dire*> as being a relation to the object. Husserl says, "*Expressions* unfold their function of
meaning [*Bedeutungsfunktion* <*function de vouloir-dire*>] even in *the solitary
life of the soul, where they no longer function as indications*. In truth therefore

---

* First Logical Investigation, §1.

the two concepts of sign are not really related to one another as concepts that are wider or narrower."[10]

Before opening this field of the solitary life of the soul in order to recover expressivity in it, it is necessary therefore to determine and reduce the domain of indication. This is what Husserl begins by doing. But before following him in this analysis, let us pause for a moment.

The movement that we just commented upon is actually open to two possible readings.

On the one hand, Husserl seems to repress, with a dogmatic haste, a question about the *structure of the sign in general.* By proposing from the start a radical dissociation between two *heterogeneous* types of sign, between indication and expression, he does not ask himself what the sign *in general* is. The concept of sign in general—which he has to use <24> at the beginning and to which he would have to grant a hearthstead of sense—is able to receive its unity only from an essence. The general concept can only be patterned on the essence. And the essence must be recognized in an essential structure of experience and in the familiarity of a horizon. In order to hear the word "sign" at the opening of the problematic, we must already have a relation of pre-understanding with the essence, the function, or the essential structure of the sign in general. Then, however, will we be able eventually to distinguish between the sign as indication and the sign as expression, even if the two types of signs are not ordered according to the relations of genus and species. According to a distinction which is itself Husserlian (cf. First Logical Investigation, §13), one can say that the category of the sign in general is not a genus but rather a form.

What therefore is a sign in general? For many reasons, our ambition is not to answer this question. We only want to suggest the sense in which Husserl may seem to evade it. "Every sign is a sign for something"— "for something" (*für etwas*), these are Husserl's first words, the words that *immediately* introduce the dissociation of expression from indication: "But not every sign has a 'Bedeutung,' a 'sense' [*Sinn*] that the sign 'expresses.'" This presupposes that we knew implicitly what "being-for" means, in the sense of "being-in-the-place-of." We must understand in a familiar way this structure of substitution or of referral so that, in this structure, the heterogeneity between indicative referral and expressive referral becomes consequently intelligible, indeed, demonstrated—and even so that the evidentness of their relations comes to be accessible for us, perhaps in the sense in which Husserl hears it. A little later (in §8), Husserl will in fact demonstrate that expressive referral (*Hinzulenken, Hinzeigen*) is not indicative referral (*Anzeigen*). But no original question is posed about *Zeigen in general,* which, pointing the finger in this way at the invisible, can then be modified into *Hinzeigen* or into *Anzeigen*. How-ever, we can already guess—and perhaps we shall later verify it—that this "Zeigen" is the place in which the root and the <25> necessity of all the "entanglements" between indication and expression are announced. "Zeigen" is the place in which all the oppositions and differences that will henceforth crisscross Husserl's analysis (and that will be wholly formed within the concepts of traditional metaphysics) are not yet sketched out. But Husserl, choosing the logicity of signification as his theme, believ-ing already that he is able to isolate the *logical a priori* from pure gram-mar within the general *a priori* of grammar, is resolutely engaged in one of the modifications of the general structure of *Zeigen: Hinzeigen* and not *Anzeigen*.

Does this absence of a question in regard to the starting point and the pre-understanding of an operative concept necessarily translate into a dogmatism? *On the other hand,* may we not interpret this as critical vigi-lance? Is not what is at issue precisely the rejection or erasure of pre-understanding as the apparent starting point, indeed, its rejection or erasure as a kind of prejudice or presumption? By what right may we presume the essential unity of something like the sign? And what if Hus-serl wanted to break up the unity of the sign, to demonstrate that it has a unity only in appearance, to reduce it to a verbality without concept? And what if there were not *one* concept of sign and *several* types of sign, but two irreducible concepts to which we have improperly attached one sole word? At the beginning of the second section, Husserl speaks precisely of "two concepts attached to the word 'sign.'" By blaming him for not beginning with an interrogation of the sign-being of the sign in general, are we not trusting in a rather hasty way the unity of a word?

More seriously, by asking *"what is* the sign in general," we subordi-nate the question of the sign to an ontological design. We claim to assign to signification a place, which might be fundamental or regional, within an ontology. This would be a classical way of proceeding. We would sub-ordinate the sign to truth, language to being, speech to thought, and writing to speech.[11] Is it not the case that, by saying that there can be a truth for the sign in general, we are assuming that the sign is not the possibility of truth, that the sign does not constitute truth, but is content to signify the truth, <26> to reproduce it, to incarnate it, and to inscribe it secondarily or to refer to it? For, if the sign somehow preceded what we call truth or essence, it would make no sense to speak of the truth or the essence of the sign. Is it not possible to think—and doubtlessly Husserl has done this—that the sign, for example if we consider the sign as the structure of an intentional movement, does not fall under the category of the thing in general (*Sache*), that the sign is not a "being" about whose being we would have just posed a question? Is not the sign something other than a being? Is it not the sole "thing" which, not being a thing, does not fall under the question of "what is"? And in contrast, does not the sign sometimes produce the question, thus produce "philosophy" as the empire of the *ti esti*?

By asserting that "logical *Bedeutung* is an expression," that there is theoretical truth only in a statement,[*] by engaging resolutely in a question concerning linguistic expression as the possibility of truth, by not presupposing the essential unity of the sign, Husserl could appear to reverse the direction of the traditional procedure and respect in the activity of signification what, having no truth in itself, conditions the movement and the concept of truth. And in fact, throughout an itinerary that ends up at "The Origin of Geometry," Husserl will give a growing attention to what in signification, in language, and in inscription as it writes ideal objectivity down, *produces* truth or ideality rather than *records* it.

But this last movement is not simple. Here is our problem and we will have to return to it. The historical destiny of phenomenology seems, no matter what, to be contained between these two motives. On the one hand, phenomenology is the reduction of naive ontology, the return to an active constitution of sense and validity, to the activity <27> of a *life* that produces truth and validity in general through its signs. But at the same time, without being simply juxtaposed to this movement,[†] another necessity confirms also the classical metaphysics of presence and indicates that phenomenology belongs to classical ontology.

We have chosen to be interested in this relation in which phenomenology belongs to classical ontology.

---

[*] This is a very frequent comment, starting with the *Logical Investigations* (cf., for example, introduction, §2) all the way up to "The Origin of Geometry."

[†] This is a movement on the basis of which we can interpret in diverse ways the relation to metaphysics and to classical ontology. It is a critique which would have determinate, limited, but certain affinities with that of Nietzsche and of Bergson. In any case, the critique belongs to the unity of a historical configuration. That this critique, in the historical configuration of these reversals, continues metaphysics is one of the most permanent themes of Heidegger's meditation. So, concerning these problems (the starting point in the pre-understanding of the sense of a word, the privilege of the question "what is," the relation between language and being or truth, the belonging to classical ontology, etc.), only on the basis of a superficial reading of Heidegger's texts could one conclude that Heidegger's texts fall under the blow of these objections. On the contrary, we think, without being able to develop it here, that no one has ever better escaped from them prior to Heidegger's texts, which does not mean that one escapes from the objections often after Heidegger's texts.

2

The Reduction of Indication

<28> That phenomenology belongs to metaphysics is revealed doubtlessly in the theme to which we are now returning: the exteriority of indication in relation to expression. Husserl devotes only three sections to *"the essence of indication"* and, in the same chapter, eleven sections are devoted to *expression*. Since, according to a logical and epistemological concern, what is at issue is to secure the originality of expression as "meaning" <*vouloir-dire*> and as the relation to an ideal object, the treatment of indication must be brief, preliminary, and "reductive." It is necessary to push indication to the side, abstract it, "reduce" it as an extrinsic and empirical phenomenon, even though a strict relation unites it in fact to expression, interweaves it empirically with expression. But such a reduction is difficult. Only in appearance does it look as though at the end of the third section the reduction is accomplished. Indicative attachments, at times of another type, will not stop appearing later, and their elimination will be an infinite task. Husserl's whole enterprise—and well beyond the *Logical Investigations*—will be threatened if the *Verflechtung* attaching indication onto expression is absolutely irreducible and in principle inextricable, if indication were not added onto expression as a more or less tenacious bond, but inhabited the essential intimacy of the movement of expression.

What is an indicative sign? First it can be *natural* (the canals of Mars *indicate* the possible presence of intelligent beings) <29> as well as *artificial* (the chalk mark, branding, all the instruments of conventional designation).* The opposition between nature and institution has no relevance

---

* In the logic of his examples and of his analysis, Husserl could have cited the *grapheme* in general. Although writing is for him—there is no doubt about it—*indicative* in its proper stratum, it poses a considerable problem which probably explains Husserl's careful silence here. Even if we suppose that writing is indicative in the sense that he gives to this word, it has a strange privilege that risks the disorganization of all the essential distinctions. What phonetic writing (or better, in the purely phonetic part of the kind of writing that is improperly and globally called phonetic) would "indicate" would be an "expression." Nonphonetic writing would be substituted for expressive discourse in such a way that nonphonetic discourse would substitute for that which unites expressive discourse immediately to the "meaning" <*vouloir-dire*> (*bedeuten*). We are not here stressing this problem, but it belongs to the ultimate horizon of this essay.

here and does not divide the unity of the indicative function. What is this unity? Husserl describes it as that of a certain "motivation" (*Motivierung*). Motivation is what gives to something like a "thinking being" the movement in order *to pass* in thought from something to something. For the moment, this definition must remain rather general. This passage can be that of conviction (*Überzeugung*) or of presumption (*Vermutung*) and it always links an *actual* knowledge right now to a *non-actual* knowledge.[1] In relation to motivation considered at this degree of generality, this knowledge can concern any object (*Gegenstand*) or state-of-affair (*Sachverhalt*) and not necessarily empirical existents, that is, individuals. In order to designate the category of the known (actual or non-actual), Husserl by design makes use therefore of very general concepts (*Sein, Bestand*) which can cover being or subsistence, the structure of ideal objects as well as empirical existents. *Sein, bestehen, Bestand*—words that are frequent and fundamental at the beginning of this section—are not to be reduced to *Dasein, existieren, Realität,* and this difference is quite important to Husserl, as we are going to verify in a moment.

Husserl thus defines the most general essential common characteristic <30> that gathers together all the indicative functions:

> In these cases we discover as a common characteristic the following situation: certain objects or *states of affairs* whatsoever whose *subsistence* [*Bestand*] of which someone has *actual* knowledge indicate [*anzeigen*] to him the *subsistence of certain other objects or states of affairs,* in the sense that *his conviction in the being [Sein] of the one is experienced as motivating (though as a non-evident motivation) a conviction or a presumption in the being* of the others.[*][2]

But this essential common characteristic is still so general that it covers the whole field of indication and something else as well. Or rather, since it is really an *Anzeigen* that is being described here, let us say that this essential common characteristic overflows indication *in the strict sense.* We are now going to have to approach this strict sense of indication. And we see then why it was important to distinguish between *Sein* and *Bestand* on the one hand, and *Existenz, Dasein,* or *Realität* on the other. General motivation thus defined is that of a "because" which can have the sense of indicative allusion (*Hinweis*) as well as that of deductive, evident, and apodictic demonstration (*Beweis*). In the latter case, the "because" links together evident and ideal necessities which are permanent and persistent beyond every empirical *hic et nunc*. Husserl says, "An ideal rule is

---

* First Logical Investigation, §2.

here revealed which extends its sway beyond the judgments linked by motivation *hic et nunc* and embraces as such in a meta-empirical generality all the judgments of like content and moreover all the judgments of like 'form' [*Form*]."[3] Motivations linking lived-experiences, the *acts* intending objective-ideal, necessary, and evident idealities may be of the order of contingent and empirical, "non-evident" indication. But the relations uniting the *contents* of ideal objects, in evidential demonstration, do not belong to indication. The entire analysis of section 3 demonstrates that (1) even if A indicates B with a complete *empirical* certainty (with the highest probability), this indication will never be a demonstration of apodictic necessity, and, to find here again the classic schema, it will never be a demonstration <31> of "truths of reason" in opposition to "truths of fact." Section 3's analysis also demonstrates (2) that even if indication seems nevertheless to intervene in a demonstration, it will always be on the side of psychical motivations, acts, convictions, etc., and never on the side of the contents of truths that are linked together.

This indispensable distinction between *Hinweis* and *Beweis*, indication and demonstration, not only poses a problem formally analogous to the one that we were opening up earlier in relation to *Zeigen*. What is monstration (*Weisen*) in general prior to its distribution into indication that points the finger (*Hinweis*) at the non-seen and into demonstration (*Beweis*) which allows something to be seen in the evidentness of the proof?[4] Also, this distinction sharpens then the difficulty of the "entanglement" that we have already pointed out.

In fact, we know now that, in the order of signification in general, every psychical lived-experience, on the side of its *acts*, even when the acts aim at idealities and objective necessities, is involved only with indicative concatenations. Indication falls outside of the content of absolutely ideal objectivity, that is, outside of the truth. Here again, this exteriority, or rather this extrinsic characteristic of indication, is inseparable, in its possibility, from the possibility of all the reductions to come, whether they are eidetic or transcendental. Having its "origin" in phenomena of association[*] <32> and always connecting empirical existents in the world,

---

[*] Cf. §4: "The psychical facts in which the notion of indication has its 'origin,' i.e., in which it can be abstractively apprehended, belong to the wider group of facts which fall under the historical rubric of the 'association of ideas.'" <Translator: First Logical Investigation, §4; the equivalent passage can be found on page 186 of the English translation, volume 1.> We know that, while renewing it and using it in the field of transcendental experience, Husserl has never stopped working with the concept of "association." Here, what is excluded from pure expressivity is indication and thereby association in the sense of empirical psychology. We must bracket empirical psychical lived-experiences in order to recognize the ideality of the *Bedeutung* that orders expression. The distinction between indication and

indicative signification will cover, in language, all of what falls under the blows of the "reductions": factuality, mundane existence, essential non-necessity, non-evidence, etc. Do we not already have the right to say that the entire future problematic of the reduction and all the conceptual differences in which they are declared (fact/essence, transcendentality/mundanity, and all the oppositions that are systematic with them) are developed in a *hiatus* between two types of signs? At the same time as the hiatus, if not in it and thanks to it? Is it not the case that the concept of *parallelism*, which defines the relations between the pure psychical—which is in the world—and the pure transcendental—which is not in the world—and which gathers together in this way the entire enigma of Husserl's phenomenology, is it not the case that this is announced here in the form of a relation between two modes of signification? And yet Husserl, who never wanted to assimilate experience in general (empirical or transcendental experience) to language, is constantly going to try to keep signification outside the self-presence of transcendental life. The question that we just raised would make us pass from commentary to interpretation. If we could answer the question in the affirmative, we would have to conclude, against Husserl's express intention, that the "reduction," even before it becomes a method, would be merged with the most spontaneous act of spoken discourse, the simple practice of speech, the power of expression. Although this conclusion must constitute in our eyes, in a certain sense, the "truth" of phenomenology, it would contradict at a certain level Husserl's express intention for two sorts of reasons. <33> On the one hand, this conclusion goes against Husserl's express intention because, as we were recalling earlier, Husserl believes in the existence of a pre-expressive and pre-linguistic stratum of sense which the reduction will at times have to unveil by excluding the stratum of language. On the other hand, if there is no expression and no meaning <*vouloir-dire*> without discourse, not all discourse is "expressive." Although there is no possible discourse without an expressive kernel, we could almost say that the totality of discourse is gripped by an indicative web.

---

expression appears therefore first of all in the necessarily and provisionally "objectivist" phase of phenomenology, when one has to neutralize empirical subjectivity. Does it keep its value when the transcendental thematic will found the analysis and when we return to constituting subjectivity? Such is the question which Husserl has never opened afterward. He has continued to make use of the "essential distinctions" from the first of the *Logical Investigations*. He has never, however, started over, repeated, in regard to them this work of thematization by which all his other concepts have been untiringly taken up, verified, constantly reappearing at the center of a description.

3

Meaning as Soliloquy

<34> Let us suppose that indication is excluded. What remains is expression. What is expression? It is a sign charged with *Bedeutung*. Husserl attempts to define it in the fifth section: *Ausdrücke als bedeutsame Zeichen*. Expressions are signs that "mean" <*veulent-dire*>.[1]

A) Doubtlessly *Bedeutung* comes upon the sign and transforms it into expression only with speech, with oral discourse. Husserl writes, "from *indicative* signs we distinguish *meaningful* signs, i.e., *expressions*." But why expressions and why "meaningful" signs <*signes ."voulant-dire"*>? We are able to explain this only by tying together a whole sheaf of reasons within the profound unity of one and the same intention.

1. Ex-pression is exteriorization. Expression imprints in a certain outside a sense which is discovered first in a certain inside. Earlier we suggested that this outside and this inside were absolutely original: the outside is neither nature, nor the world, nor a real exteriority in relation to consciousness. Here is the place to specify this outside. The *bedeuten* intends an outside which is that of an ideal ob-ject. This outside then is ex-pressed, passes outside of itself into another outside, which is still "in" consciousness. As we are going to see, expressive discourse has no need, as such and in its essence, of being factually uttered in the world. Expression as a meaningful sign <*signe voulant-dire*> <35> is therefore a double exiting of sense (*Sinn*) outside of itself in itself, in consciousness, in the with-itself and the nearby-itself that Husserl begins by determining as the "solitary life of the soul."[2] Later, after the discovery of the transcendental reduction, he will describe the solitary life of the soul as the noetico-noematic sphere of consciousness. If we refer, in anticipation and for the sake of more clarity, to the corresponding sections of *Ideas I*, we see how the "unproductive" stratum of expression comes to reflect, "to mirror" (*widerzuspiegeln*) every other intentionality in regard to its form and to its content. The relation to objectivity therefore indicates a "pre-expressive" (*vor-ausdrücklich*) intentionality that aims at a sense which will be then transformed into a *Bedeutung* and an expression. It is not at all obvious that this reflected and repeated "exiting" toward the noematic sense and then toward expression is an unproductive redoubling, especially if we consider that by "unproductivity" Husserl intends

thus a *"productivity that is exhausted in the expressing and in the form of the conceptual* which is introduced with the expression."*,[3] Therefore we will have to return to this. We only wanted to note here what "expression" means according to Husserl: the exiting of an act outside of itself, then of a sense which is able to remain in itself only in the voice, in the "phenomenological" voice.

2. In the *Logical Investigations,* the word "expression" is already imposed for another reason. Expression is an intentional, thoroughly conscious, decided, voluntary exteriorization. There is no expression without the intention of a subject animating the sign, endowing it with *Geistigkeit.* In indication, animation has two limits: the body of the sign which is not a breath, and the indicated, which is an existence in the world. In expression, the intention is absolutely on purpose <36> because it animates a voice which can remain wholly internal and because the expressed is a *Bedeutung,* that is, an ideality that does not "exist" in the world.

3. Looking at it from another viewpoint will confirm that there can be no expression without a voluntary intention. In fact, expression is always inhabited, animated by a *bedeuten,* as a *wanting-*to-say *<vouloir-dire>,* because for Husserl the *Deutung,* let us say, the interpretation, the understanding, or the cognition, of the *Bedeutung* can never have taken place outside of oral discourse (*Rede*). Only such a discourse can make itself available to a *Deutung.* The latter is never essentially a reading but rather a hearing. What "wants to say," *what* the "meaning" wants to say, the *Bedeutung,* is reserved for the one who speaks and who speaks insofar as he says what he *wants* to say: on purpose, explicitly, and consciously. Let us verify this.

Husserl recognizes that his use of the word "expression" "constrains" the language a little. But the constraint which is thus practiced purifies his intention and at once reveals a common stock of metaphysical implications. Husserl writes, "We shall lay down, for provisional intelligibility, that each discourse [*Rede*] or part of discourse [*Redeteil*], as also each sign that is essentially of the same sort, shall count as an expression, whether or not such discourse is actually uttered [*wirklich geredet*], or addressed with communicative intent to any persons or not."[4] Thus all of what constitutes the actuality of what is uttered, the physical incarnation of the *Bedeutung,* the body of speech, which in its ideality belongs to an empirically determinate language, is, if not outside of discourse, at least for-

---

* *Ideas I,* §124. Elsewhere we analyze more directly the problematic of "wanting-to-say" and expression in *Ideas I.* See "La forme et le vouloir-dire: Note sur la phénoménologie du langage," in *Revue internationale de philosophie,* Sept. 1967.

eign to expressivity as such, to this pure intention without which no discourse would be possible. The entire stratum of empirical actuality, that is, the factual totality of discourse, belongs to this indication, the extent of which we have not finished recognizing. The actuality, the totality of these events of discourse, is not only indicative because it is in the world, abandoned to the world, but also, correlatively, because, as <37> such, the actuality of discourse keeps in itself something of *involuntary* association. For if intentionality has never simply meant will <*volonté*>, it indeed seems that in the order of the lived-experiences of expression (supposing that it has limits) intentional consciousness and voluntary consciousness are, in Husserl's eyes, synonyms. And if we were just thinking—as Husserl will authorize in *Ideas I*—that every intentional lived-experience can in principle be taken up into a lived-experience of expression, we should perhaps conclude that, despite all the themes of receptive or intuitive intentionality and of passive genesis, the concept of intentionality is still taken in the tradition of a voluntaristic metaphysics, that is, perhaps taken simply in *the* metaphysics. The explicit teleology that orders all of transcendental phenomenology would basically be only a transcendental voluntarism. Sense wants to signify itself; it expresses itself only in a wanting-to-say which is only a wanting-to-say-itself of the presence of sense.

This explains that all of what escapes from pure spiritual intention, from pure animation by the *Geist* which is the will, all of that is excluded from *bedeuten* and therefore from expression: for example, facial expressions, the various gestures, the totality of the body and of mundane registration, in a word, the totality of the visible as such and of the spatial as such. As such—that is, insofar as they are not worked over by *Geist*, by the will, by the *Geistigkeit* which, in the word as well as in the human body, transforms the *Körper* into *Leib* (into flesh). The opposition of the soul and the body is not only at the center of this doctrine of signification, it is confirmed by the doctrine and, as it has always basically been done in philosophy, the opposition depends on an interpretation of language. Visibility as such and spatiality as such could only lose the self-presence of the will and of the spiritual animation which opens up discourse. *They are literally the death of that self-presence.* Thus, as Husserl writes,

> Such a definition excludes [from expression] facial expressions and
> the various gestures which <38> involuntarily [*unwillkürlich*] accompany
> speech without communicative intent, or those in which a person's
> psychic states achieve understandable "expression" for his environment,
> without the added help of discourse. Such "externalizations" [*Äusserungen*]
> are not expressions in the sense of discourse [*Rede*], they have no
> phenomenal unity, in the consciousness of the one who externalizes

himself, with the externalized lived-experiences. By means of them, an individual communicates nothing to another. In the externalization of these lived-experiences by means of them, the intention to expose some "thought" in an express way [*in ausdrücklicher Weise*] is missing, whether for the individual himself, in his solitary state, or for others. Such "expressions," in short, have properly speaking no *Bedeutung*.[5]

They do not want *to say* anything because they do not *want* to say anything. In the order of signification, the express intention is an intention to express. The implicit does not belong to the essence of discourse. What Husserl asserts here concerning gestures and facial expressions would of course have to hold *a fortiori* for preconscious or unconscious language.

That we may eventually "interpret" the gesture, the facial expression, the non-conscious, the involuntary, indication in general, that we may at times take them up and make them explicit in a discursive and express commentary, that only confirms, in Husserl's eyes, the preceding distinctions. This interpretation (*Deutung*) makes a latent expression be *heard,* a wanting-to-say (*bedeuten <vouloir-dire>*) which was still holding itself in reserve. Non-expressive signs want to say (*bedeuten*) only insofar as one can make them say what was murmuring in them, what was wanting to be said in a sort of mumbling. Gestures want to say only insofar as we can listen to them, interpret them (*deuten*). As long as we identify *Sinn* and *Bedeutung*, all of what resists the *Deutung* has no sense and is not language in the strict sense. The essence of language is its *telos* and its *telos* is voluntary consciousness as wanting-to-say. The indicative sphere which remains outside <39> expressivity so defined demarcates the failure of this *telos*. The indicative sphere represents all of what, while interweaving itself with expression, cannot be taken up into a deliberate discourse that is permeated by wanting-to-say.

For all of these reasons, we do not have the right to distinguish between indication and expression as between a non-linguistic sign and a linguistic sign. Husserl traces out a border which does not pass between language and non-language, but, within language in general, between the express and the non-express (with all of their connotations). For it would be difficult—and *in fact* impossible—to exclude from language all the indicative forms. At most, we can therefore distinguish with Husserl between linguistic signs "in the strict sense" and linguistic signs in the broad sense. Justifying his exclusion of gestures and facial expression, Husserl in effect concludes:

It is not to the point that another person may interpret [*deuten*] our involuntary externalizations [*unwillkürlichen Äusserungen*], e.g., our

"expressive movements," and that he may thereby become deeply ac-
quainted with our inner thoughts and emotions. They (these externalizations) "want to say" [*bedeuten*] something to him insofar as he inter-
prets [*deutet*] them, but even for him they have no *Bedeutungen* in the
strict sense of linguistic signs [*im prägnanten Sinne sprachlicher Zeichen*],
but only in the sense of indicating.*,6

This leads us to look for the limit of the indicative field still farther.
In fact, even for the one who restores the discursivity in the gestures
of others, the indicative manifestations of others are not transformed
into expressions. It is the interpreter who expresses himself in regard to
them. Perhaps there is something in the relation to others that makes
indication irreducible.

B) In fact, it is not enough to recognize oral discourse as the milieu of expressivity. Once we have excluded all the non-discursive signs
which are given immediately as exterior to speech (gestures, facial expressions), still <40> we find, this time within speech, a non-expressivity
whose scope is considerable. This non-expressivity is not only based on
the physical side of expression ("the sensible sign, the articulate phonic
complex, the sign written on paper"). Husserl writes, "The simple distinction between physical signs and sense-giving lived-experiences in general
is by no means enough, and not at all enough for logical purposes."7

Considering now the non-physical side of discourse, Husserl therefore excludes from it, always under the heading of indication, all that
arises from the *communication* or from the *manifestations* of psychical lived-
experience. The movement that justifies this exclusion should teach us
a lot about the metaphysical tenor of this phenomenology. The themes
which are presented here will never be put back into question by Husserl.
On the contrary, they will constantly get confirmed. They are going to
make us think that what, in the final analysis, separates expression from
indication is what we could call the immediate non-self-presence of the
living present. The values of mundane existence, naturality, sensibility,
empiricity, association, etc., which determined the concept of indication,
are perhaps—across of course many mediations that we are anticipat-
ing—going to find their final unity in this non-presence. And this non-
self-presence of the living present will qualify simultaneously the relation
to others in general and the self-relation of temporalization.

This is sketched out slowly, discretely, but rigorously in the *Logical
Investigations*. We have seen that the difference between indication and

---

* First Logical Investigation, §5

expression was functional or intentional but not substantial. Husserl can therefore consider that the elements of the order that is substantially discursive (words, the parts of discourse in general) function in certain cases as indications. And this indicative function of discourse is massively at work. *All discourse, insofar as it is engaged in a communication and insofar as it manifests lived-experiences, operates as indication.* In this case, words act like gestures. Or <41> rather, the very concept of gesture should be determined on the basis of indication as non-expressivity.

Husserl admits, of course, that the function for which expression is "originally framed" is communication.*,8 And yet expression is never purely itself insofar as it fulfills this originative function. Only when communication is suspended is pure expressivity able to appear.

What in fact happens in communication? Sensible (audible or visible, etc.) phenomena are animated by the acts of a subject who endows them with sense, and simultaneously another subject must understand the animating subject's intention. Now "animation" cannot be pure and total. It must traverse the non-diaphaneity of a body and in a certain way be lost there. Husserl writes,

> But this communication becomes a possibility if the auditor also understands the speaker's intention. He does this inasmuch as he takes the speaker to be a person, who is not merely uttering sounds but *speaking to him,* who is accompanying those sounds with certain sense-giving acts, which the sounds reveal to the hearer, or whose sense they seek to communicate to him. What first makes spiritual exchange possible, and turns connected discourse into a discourse, lies in the correlation among corresponding physical and psychic lived-experiences of communicating persons which is mediated by the physical side of speech.9

Everything in my discourse which is destined to manifest a lived-experience to another person must pass through the mediation of the physical side. This irreducible mediation involves every expression in an indicative operation. The manifestation function (*kundgebende Funktion*) is an indicative function. Here we are drawing near to the root of indication: there is indication each time that an act endowing sense, the animating intention, the living spirituality of a meaning <*vouloir-dire*>, is not fully present. In effect, when I listen to another person, his lived-experience is not present to me "in person" and originally. I can have, <42> Husserl thinks, an originary intuition, that is, an immediate

---

* First Logical Investigation, §7.

perception, of what is exposed of that person in the world, the visibility of his body, his gestures, a perception of what lets itself be heard from the sounds that he utters. But the subjective side of his experience, his consciousness, the acts by which in particular he endows sense to the signs, are not immediately and originarily present as they are for him and as mine are for me. Here we have an irreducible and definitive limit. The lived-experience of another becomes manifest to me only insofar as it is mediately indicated by the signs involving a physical side. The very idea of the "physical," of the "physical side," can only be thought in its proper difference on the basis of this movement of indication.

In order to explain the irreducibly indicative character of manifestation, even in discourse, Husserl already proposes motives whose system the fifth of the *Cartesian Meditations* will develop minutely. Outside of the transcendental monadic sphere of my own (*mir eigenes*), outside of the propriety of my own (*Eigenheit*), of my presence to myself, I have with what another owns, with the other's presence to himself, only relations of *analogical appresentation,* relations of *mediate and potential intentionality*. Originary presentation is forbidden to me. What will be described then under the watchful eye of a differentiated, audacious, and rigorous transcendental reduction is here in the *Logical Investigations* sketched out in the "parallel" dimension of the psychical. Husserl writes,

> The hearer perceives the manifestation in the same sense in which he perceives the very person who manifests—even though the psychic phenomena which make him a person cannot fall, for what they are, in the intuitive grasp of another. Common language credits us with percepts even of other people's psychic lived-experiences; we "see" their anger, their pain, etc. Such talk is quite correct, as long as, e.g., we allow outward bodily things likewise to count as perceived, and as long as, in general, the notion of <43> perception is not restricted to adequate perception, to intuition in the strict sense. If the essential characteristic of perception lies in the intuitive intention [*Vermeinen*] claiming to grasp a thing or an event insofar as they are themselves present [*gegenwärtigen*]—such an intention is possible, and it is even given in the immense majority of cases without any conceptual or express formulation—then the grasping of the manifestation [*Kundnahme*] is a simple perception of the manifestation [*Kundgabe*]. . . . The hearer perceives the fact that the one who is speaking is externalizing certain psychic lived-experiences, and to that extent he also perceives these lived-experiences. He does not, however, live them himself; he has no "internal" perception of them, only an "external" perception. Here we have the big difference between the actual grasp of a being in

adequate intuition, and the intended [*vermeintlichen*] grasp of a being
upon the foundation of an intuitive but inadequate representation. In
the former case, we have to do with a being given in lived-experience, in
the latter case with a presumed [*supponiertes*] being, to which no truth
corresponds at all. Mutual understanding demands a certain correlation among the psychic acts which are unfolded from the two sides of
manifestation and in the grasping of the manifestation, but not at all
their full identity.[10]

The notion of *presence* is the nerve of this demonstration. If communication or manifestation (*Kundgabe*) is essentially indicative, it is so because the presence of the other's lived-experience is denied to our originary intuition. Each time that the immediate and full presence of the
signified will be stolen away, the signifier will be of an indicative nature.
(This is why *Kundgabe,* which we are translating loosely by "manifestation," does not manifest, renders nothing manifest, if manifest means
evident, open, offered "in person." *Kundgabe* announces and at the same
time snatches away what it is informing us about.) All discourse, or rather,
all of what, in discourse, does not restore the immediate presence of the
signified content, is in-expressive. Pure expressivity will be the pure active intention (spirit, psyche, life, will) of a <44> *bedeuten* that is animating
a discourse whose content (*Bedeutung*) will be present. It is present not
in nature, since indication alone takes place in nature and in space, but in
consciousness. Therefore it is present to an "internal" intuition or to an
"internal" perception. But we just understood why it is present to an intuition that is not that of the other in a case of communication. Therefore
this is *self-present* in the life of a present that has still not exited from itself
into the world, into space, into nature. With all of these "exitings" exiling
this life of self-presence into indication, we can be sure that indication,
which covers so far nearly the entire surface of language, is the process
of death at work in the signs. And as soon as the other appears, indicative
language—which is another name of the relation to death—no longer
lets itself be erased.

The relation to the other as non-presence is therefore the impurity of expression. In order to reduce indication in language and attain
once more finally pure expressivity, it is therefore necessary to suspend
the relation to others. Then I would no longer have to pass through the
mediation of the physical side or through any appresentation in general.
Section 8, "Expressions in the Solitary Life of the Soul," follows therefore
a path which, from two viewpoints, is parallel to the path of the reduction
to the monadic sphere of *Eigenheit* in the *Cartesian Meditations:* the parallel of the psychical and the transcendental, and the parallel of the stra-

tum of expressive lived-experiences and the stratum of lived-experiences in general. Husserl says,

> So far we have considered expressions as used in communication, which last depend essentially on the fact that they operate indicatively. But expressions also play a great part in the life of the soul insofar as it is not engaged in a relation of communication. This change in function plainly has nothing to do with whatever makes an expression an expression. Expressions continue to have their *Bedeutungen* as they had before, and the same *Bedeutungen* as in dialogue. A word only ceases to be a word when our interest is directed exclusively on <45> the sensible, when it becomes a simple phonic form. But when we live in the understanding of a word, it expresses something and the same thing, whether we address it to anyone or not. It seems clear, therefore, that an expression's *Bedeutung*, and what yet belongs to it essentially, cannot coincide with its activity of manifestation.[11]

The first advantage of this reduction to the interior monologue is therefore that the physical event of language seems to be indeed absent from interior monologue. To the extent that the unity of the word—what makes it recognizable as a word, as *the same* word, the unity of a phonic complex and a sense—cannot be merged with the multiplicity of the sensible events of its employment nor does it depend on them, the *sameness* of the word is ideal. It is the ideal possibility of repetition and it loses nothing with the reduction of *any,* and therefore of *every* empirical event marked by its appearance. While "what we are to use as an indication [the distinctive sign] must be perceived by us as an existent,"[12] the unity of a word owes nothing to its *existence (Dasein, Existenz)*. Its expressivity, which does not need an empirical body but only the ideal and identical form of this body insofar as it is animated by a wanting-to-say, owes nothing to any mundane, empirical, etc. existence. In "the solitary life of the soul," the pure unity of expression as such should therefore finally be restored to me.

Is this to say that in speaking to myself I communicate nothing to myself? Is it the case that then the "Kundgabe" and the "Kundnahme" are suspended? Is it the case that non-presence is reduced and with it indication, analogical detour, etc.? Do I then no longer modify myself? Is it the case that I learn nothing about myself?

Husserl considers the objection and then sets it aside: "Shall one say that one who speaks in solitude to himself, and that for him also the words serve as signs [*Zeichen*], namely, indications [*Anzeichen*] of his own psychic lived-experiences? I do not think that such a view must be held."[13]

<46> Husserl's argumentation here is decisive and we must follow it closely. The whole theory of signification announced in this first chapter of essential distinctions would collapse if a function of *Kundgabe/Kundnahme* would not let itself be reduced in the sphere of my own lived-experiences, and if overall the ideal or absolute solitude of "proper" subjectivity still needed indications in order to constitute its own self-relation. And fundamentally let us not deceive ourselves here: the need for indications means quite simply the need for signs. For it is more and more clear that, despite the initial distinction between the indicative sign and the expressive sign, only indication is truly a sign for Husserl. Full expression—that is, as we shall see later, the fulfilled intention of the meaning—in a certain way, escapes from the concept of sign. Already in the sentence that we just cited from Husserl, we could read: "signs, namely, indications." But let us still consider that as a slip of the tongue whose truth will be revealed only later. Instead of saying "signs, namely, indications" (*als Zeichen, nämlich als Anzeichen*), let us say: "signs, namely, signs in the form of indications." For on the surface of his text, Husserl continues to respect for the moment the initial distinction between two sorts of signs.

In order to demonstrate that indication no longer functions in the solitary life of the soul, Husserl begins by marking the difference between two kinds of "referral": referral as *Hinzeigen* (which we must keep from translating as indication, at least for conventional reasons and if we do not want to destroy the coherence of the text; let us say arbitrarily "monstration") and referral as *Anzeigen* (indication). Now, as Husserl writes, if in silent monologue "words function as signs here as they do everywhere," and if "everywhere we can speak simply of an act of monstration [*Hinzeigen*],"[14] then the transgression of expression toward sense, of the signifier toward the signified, is here no longer an indication. The *Hinzeigen* is not an *Anzeigen*. For this transgression or, if you like, here this referral <47> does without all existence (*Dasein, Existenz*). In contrast, in indication, an existing sign, an empirical event refers to a content whose existence is at least presumed. It motivates our anticipation or our conviction of the existence of what is indicated. We cannot think indication without making the category of empirical, that is, merely probable, existence intervene, and this will also be the definition of mundane existence for Husserl in opposition to the existence of the *ego cogito*. The reduction to monologue is really a bracketing of empirical, mundane existence. In the "solitary life of the soul," we no longer make use of *real* (*wirklich*) words, but only of *represented* (*vorgestellt*) words. And lived-experience—about which we were wondering if it was not itself "indicated" to the speaking subject—does not have to be thus indicated; it is immediately certain and self-present. While in real communication, existing signs *indicate* other existents which are only probable and mediately evoked, in monologue, when the expression is *full*,*,15 non-existent signs *show* <48> the signifieds (*Bedeutungen*), which are ideal and therefore non-existent, and certain, for they are present to intuition. As for the certainty of internal existence, it has no need, Husserl thinks, of being signified. It is immediately present to itself. It is living consciousness.

In interior monologue, the word would therefore be merely represented. Its place can be the imaginary (*Phantasie*). We are content to imagine the word whose existence is in this way neutralized. In this imagination of the word, in this imaginary representation of the word (*Phantasievorstellung*), we no longer need the empirical event of the word. We are indifferent to its existence or non-existence. For if we need then the *imagination* of the word, at the same time we do without the *imagined word*. The imagination of the word, the imagined, the imagined-being of the word, its "image," is not the (imagined) word. Just as in the perception of the word, the (perceived or appearing) word which is "in the world" belongs to a radically different order from that of the perception or the appearing of the word, the perceived-being of the word, likewise the (imagined) word is of a radically heterogeneous order from that of the imagination of the word. This difference, which is at once simple and subtle, makes the irreducible specificity of phenomenality appear. We are able to understand nothing of phenomenology if we do not pay constant and vigilant attention to this specificity.

But why is Husserl not satisfied with the difference between the exi ,ting (perceived) word and the perception or the perceived being, the

---

* In order not to confuse and multiply the difficulties, we are considering here in this precise place only perfect expressions, that is, the ones for which the "Bedeutungsinten- tion" is "fulfilled." We are authorized to do this insofar as this fullness, as we shall see, is the *telos* and the achievement of what Husserl wants here to isolate under the name of wanting-to-say and expression. Non-fulfillment will bring to the surface originary problems to which we shall return below.

Let us cite the passage which supports what we were just saying: "But if we reflect on the relation of expression and *Bedeutung,* and to this end break up our complex, intimately unified lived-experience of the expression fulfilled with sense, into the two factors of word and sense, the word comes before us intrinsically indifferent, whereas the sense seems the thing aimed at by the verbal sign, and meant by its means: the expression seems to direct interest away from itself towards its sense [*von sich ab und auf den Sinn hinzulenken*], and to refer [*hinzuzeigen*] to the latter. But this reference [*Hinzeigen*] is not an indication [*das Anzei- gen*] in the sense previously discussed. The existence [*Dasein*] of the sign neither 'motivates' the existence of the meaning, nor, properly expressed, our conviction in the existence of the *Bedeutung.* What we are to use as an indication [the distinctive sign] must be perceived by us as existent [*als daseiend*]. This holds also of expressions used in communicative dis- course, but not for expressions used in solitary discourse" (First Logical Investigation, §8).

phenomenon of the word? It is because in the phenomenon of perception, a reference is located in phenomenality itself to the existence of the
word. The sense "existence" belongs then to the phenomenon. This is
no longer the case in the phenomenon of imagination. In imagination,
the existence of the word is not implied, not even by means of the intentional sense. What then *exists* is only the imagination of the word, which is
itself absolutely certain and self-present insofar as it is a lived-experience.
What we already have here is a phenomenological reduction, that isolates
the subjective lived-experience as the <49> sphere of absolute certainty
and absolute existence. This absolute of existence appears only in the
reduction of existence that is relative to the transcendent world. And it
is already imagination, "the vital element of phenomenology" (*Ideas I*),[16]
which gives this movement its privileged medium. Husserl writes,

> Here [in solitary discourse], we are in general content with represented
> words rather than with real words. In imagination, a spoken or printed
> word floats before us, though in reality it has no existence. We should
> not, however, confuse imaginative representations [*Phantasievorstellun-
> gen*], and still less the contents of imagination on which they rest, with
> their imagined objects. The imagined verbal sound, or the imagined
> printed word, does not exist, only its imaginative representation does
> so. The difference is the difference between imagined centaurs and the
> imagination of such beings. The word's non-existence [*Nicht-Existenz*]
> neither disturbs nor interests us, since it leaves the word's expressive
> function unaffected.[17]

This argumentation would be very fragile if it appealed only to a
classical psychology of imagination. And it would be really unwise to understand it in this way. For such a psychology, the image is a picture-sign
whose *reality* (whether it is physical or psychical) indicates the imagined
object. Husserl will show in *Ideas I* how such a conception leads to aporias.*

---

* Cf. §90 and the entire chapter 4 of part 3, in particular §§99, 109, 111, and especially 112: "This
will only be changed when there will be more extensive practice in genuine phenomenological analysis than heretofore has been the case. As long as one deals with lived-experiences as
'contents' or as psychical 'elements' which are still regarded as bits of things [*Sächelchen*] despite all the fashionable arguments against atomizing and physicalizing psychology, as long
as one believes that he has found, accordingly, the distinction between 'sensation-contents'
and corresponding 'fantasy-contents' only in the material traits of 'intensity,' 'fullness,' or
the like, there can be no improvement. One must first learn to see that at issue here is a difference pertaining to consciousness." <Translator: The equivalent passage can be found on
pages 262–63 of the Kersten English translation.> The phenomenological originality that
Husserl wants thus to respect leads him to posit an absolute heterogeneity between percep-

Insofar as it is the intentional sense <50> or noema, and although it belongs to the sphere of the existence and absolute certainty of consciousness, the image is not a reality duplicating another reality. This is the case not only because the image is not a reality (*Realität*) in nature, but also because the noema is a non-reell (*reell*) component of consciousness.

Saussure was also careful to distinguish between the real word and its image. He acknowledged the expressive value of the "signifier" solely in the form of the "acoustic image."*,18 <51> "Signifier" means "acoustic

---

tion or originary presentation (*Gegenwärtigung, Präsentation*) and re-presentation or representative re-production, which we also translate by presentification (*Vergegenwärtigung*). Memory, the image, the sign are re-presentations in this sense. Truly, Husserl is not *led* to acknowledge this heterogeneity. This heterogeneity constitutes the whole possibility of phenomenology which makes sense only if a pure and originary presentation is possible and original. Therefore, although we cannot study here directly the complex and fundamental system of such a distinction (to which we must add, at the least, the distinction between positional [*setzende*] re-presentation and imaginary re-presentation [*Phantasie-Vergegenwärtigung*] which is neutral in this regard), it is therefore the indispensable instrument for a criticism of classical psychology, and in particular for a criticism of the classical psychology of the imagination and of the sign. But, is it not the case that we are able to take this criticism of naive psychology only up to a certain point? And are we not able to show finally that the theme and value of "pure presentation," of originary and pure perception, of full and simple presence, etc., constitute the complicity of phenomenology with classical psychology, their common metaphysical presupposition? By asserting that *perception does not exist* or that what we call perception is not originary, and that in a certain way everything "begins" by means of "re-presentation" (this is a proposition which obviously can be sustained only within the erasure of these last two concepts; this proposition means that there is no "beginning" and the "re-presentation" of which we are speaking is not the modification of a "re" that has *supervened* upon an originary presentation), by re-inserting the difference of the "sign" in the heart of the "originary," what is at issue is not to turn back away from transcendental phenomenology—and it does not matter whether this turning back would be toward an "empiricism" or toward a "Kantian" critique of the claim to an originary intuition. In this way we have just designated the primary intention—and the distant horizon—of the present essay.

* It is necessary to put the following passage of the *Course in General Linguistics* side by side with the text of the *Logical Investigations:* "The linguistic sign is not a link between a thing and a name, but between a concept and an acoustic image. The acoustic image is not actually a sound; for a sound is something physical. The acoustic image is the hearer's psychological impression of a sound, a representation as given to him by the evidence of his senses. The acoustic image may be called a 'material' element only in that it is the representation of our sensory impression. The acoustic image may thus be distinguished from the other element associated with it in a linguistic sign. This other element is generally of a more abstract kind: the concept. The psychological nature of our acoustic images becomes clear when we consider our own linguistic activity. *Without moving either lips or tongue, we can speak to ourselves or recite silently a piece of verse*" (*Course in General Linguistics*, page 66; my italics). And Saussure adds this warning that we have really quickly forgotten: "We grasp the words of a language as acoustic images. That is why it is best to avoid referring to them as composed of the 'phonemes' that make up the words. Such a term, implying the activity

image." But since Saussure does not take the "phenomenological" precaution, he turns the acoustic image, the signifier as a "psychical impression," into a reality whose sole originality is to be interior; by doing this, he only moves the problem to a different place. Now, if Husserl, in the *Logical Investigations,* leads his description into a psychical and not transcendental zone, he then nevertheless discerns the essential components of a structure that he will delineate in *Ideas I:* phenomenal lived-experience does not belong to reality (*Realität*). In phenomenal lived-experience, certain elements belong in a reell manner (*reell*) to consciousness (*hyle, morphē,* and *noesis*), but the noematic content, the <52> sense is a non-reell (*reell*) component of the lived-experience.* The irreality of internal discourse is therefore a very differentiated structure. Husserl very precisely writes, although without emphasis:

> . . . a spoken or printed word floats before us, though in reality, it has no existence. We should not, however, confuse imaginative representations [*Phantasievorstellungen*], *and still less* [my emphasis] the contents of imagination on which they rest, with their imagined objects.[19]

Therefore, not only does the imagination of the word, which is not the imagined word, not exist, but the *content* (the noema) of this imagination exists *still less* than the act.

---

of the vocal apparatus, is appropriate to the spoken word, to the realization of the inner image in discourse." This warning has been forgotten, but this is probably so because the proposition that Saussure advances as a replacement only aggravates the risk: "Speaking of the *sounds* and *syllables* of a word need not give rise to any misunderstanding, provided that one always bears in mind that the names refer to the acoustic image." We must of course acknowledge that it is easier to remember that warning when we speak of the phoneme than when we speak of the sound. The sound is thought outside of any real vocal activity only insofar as we situate it as an object in nature, and this situating in nature is done more easily with the sound than with the phoneme.

In order to avoid these misunderstandings, Saussure concludes in this way: "The ambiguity would be removed if these three notions in question were designated by terms which are related but contrasted. We propose to keep the term *sign* to designate the whole, but to replace *concept* and *acoustic image* respectively by *signified* and *signifier*" (*Course in General Linguistics*, page 67). We could posit the equivalence signifier/expression, signified/*Bedeutung*, if the structure *bedeuten/Bedeutung*/sense/object were not a lot more complex in Husserl than in Saussure. Also it would be necessary to compare systematically the operation to which Husserl proceeds in the First Logical Investigation to the delimitation by Saussure of the "internal system" of language.

* Concerning the non-reality of the noema in the case of the image and the sign, see, in particular, *Ideas I,* §102.

4

Meaning and Representation

<53> Let us recall the objective and nerve of this demonstration: the pure function of expression and of meaning <*vouloir-dire*> lies not in communicating, informing, manifesting, that is, not in indicating. Now, the "solitary life of the soul" would prove that this kind of expression without indication is possible. In solitary discourse, the subject learns nothing about himself, manifests nothing to himself. In order to sustain this demonstration, whose consequences will be limitless in phenomenology, Husserl appeals to two types of arguments.

1. In internal discourse, I communicate nothing to myself. I indicate nothing to myself. I can at most imagine myself doing that, I can merely represent myself as manifesting something to myself. Here we have only a *representation* and an *imagination*.

2. In internal discourse, I communicate nothing to myself and I can only pretend to, *because I have no need to communicate anything to myself.* Such an operation—communication from self to self—cannot take place because it would make no sense. And it would make no sense because it would have *no purpose.* The existence of psychical acts does not have to be indicated (recall that only an existence can in general be indicated) because the existence of psychical acts is immediately present to the subject in the present instant.

<54> Let us first read the paragraph that ties together the *two arguments:*

> One of course *speaks,* in a certain sense, even in solitary discourse, and it is certainly possible to think of oneself as speaking, and even as speaking to oneself, as, for example, when someone says to himself: "you have gone wrong, you can't go on like that." But in the genuine sense of communication, there is no speech in such cases, nor does one tell oneself anything: one merely represents oneself [*man stellt sich vor*] as speaking and communicating. In a monologue words can perform no function of indicating the existence [*Dasein*] of psychic acts, since such indication would there be quite purposeless [*ganz zwecklos wäre*]. For the acts in question are themselves lived by us at that very instant [*im selben Augenblick*].[1]

These assertions raise very diverse questions. But they concern the entire status of *representation* in language. Here we have to consider representation in the general sense of *Vorstellung*, but also in the sense of representation as the repetition or reproduction of presentation, as *Vergegenwärtigung* modifying *Präsentation* or *Gegenwärtigung*. Finally we have to consider the sense of a representative taking the place of, occupying the place of another *Vorstellung* (*Repräsentation, Repräsentant, Stellverstreter*).*,2

Let us first consider the *first argument*. In monologue, we communicate nothing to ourselves; one represents oneself (*man stellt sich vor*) as being a speaking and communicating subject. Husserl here seems to apply to language the fundamental distinction between reality and representation. Between actual communication (indication) and "represented" communication, there would be an essential difference, a simple exteriority. Moreover, in order to gain access to <55> internal language (in the sense of communication) as pure representation (*Vorstellung*), we would have to pass through fiction, that is, through a particular type of representation: the imaginary representation that Husserl will define later as neutralizing representation (*Vergegenwärtigung*).

Can we apply this system of distinctions to language? First, we would have to assume that in communication, in the so-called "actual" practice of language, representation (in all the senses of this word) would not be essential and constitutive. We would have to assume that representation is only an accident added contingently onto the practice of discourse. Now, there are grounds for thinking that in language representation and reality are not added together here and there, for the simple reason that it is impossible in principle to distinguish them rigorously. And no doubt we must not say that that impossibility is produced *in* language. Language in general *is* that impossibility—by means of itself alone.

Husserl himself provides us with the means to argue for that against him. In fact, when I, *actually*, as we say, make use of words, whether I do this for communicative purposes or not (let us place ourselves here prior to this distinction and in the case of the sign in general), from the start I must operate (in) a structure of repetition whose element can only be representative. A sign is never an event if event means an empirical singularity that is irreplaceable and irreversible. A sign that would take place only "once" would not be a sign. A purely idiomatic sign would not be a sign. A signifier (in general) must be recognizable in its form despite

---

* See on this subject the note by the French translators of the *Logical Investigations* (*Recherches logiques*, vol. 2, part 1, p. 276) and that by the French translators of *The Phenomenology of the Consciousness of Internal Time* (*Leçons*, p. 26).

and across the diversity of the empirical characteristics that can modify it. It must remain the *same* and be able to be repeated as such despite and across the deformations that what we call the empirical event makes it necessarily undergo. A phoneme or grapheme is necessarily always other, to a certain extent, each time that it is presented in a procedure or a perception, but it can function as a sign and as language in general only <56> if a formal identity allows it to be reissued and to be recognized. This identity is necessarily ideal. It therefore necessarily implies a representation, as *Vorstellung*, the place of ideality in general, as *Vergegenwärtigung*, the possibility of reproductive repetition in general, as *Repräsentation*, insofar as each signifying event is a substitute (of the signified as well as of the ideal form of the signifier). Since this representative structure is signification itself, I cannot open up an "actual" discourse without being originarily engaged in an indefinite representativity.

Perhaps someone will object to us that Husserl wants precisely to bring to light this exclusively representative character of expressivity by means of his hypothesis of a solitary discourse which would respond to the essence of discourse by dropping the communicative and indicative shell. This person might continue by saying that we have formulated our question precisely with Husserlian concepts. Of course. But the point is that Husserl wants to describe only the way that expression, and not signification in general, belongs to the order of representation as *Vorstellung*. Now we just suggested that representation as *Vorstellung* and its other representative modifications are implied by every sign in general. On the other hand and especially, as soon as we admit that discourse belongs essentially to the order of representation, the distinction between "actual" discourse and discursive representation becomes suspect, whether the discourse is purely "expressive" or engaged in a "communication." By reason of the originarily repetitive structure of the sign in general, there is every chance for "actual" language to be as imaginary as imaginary discourse and for imaginary discourse to be as actual as actual discourse. Whether what is at issue is expression or indicative communication, the difference between reality and representation, between the true and the imaginary, between simple presence and repetition has always already started to erase itself. Does not the maintenance of this difference—in the history of metaphysics and still in Husserl—respond <57> to the obstinate desire to save presence and to reduce the sign or to make it be derivative? And with the sign all the potencies of repetition? This is as well to live *in* the—assured, secured, constituted—effect of repetition, of representation, in the effect of the difference which snatches presence away. To assert, as we have just done, that in the sign *the difference does not take place* between reality and representation, etc., amounts to saying therefore that the gesture that sanctions this difference is the very erasure of the sign. But there are two ways to erase the originality of the sign, and we must be attentive to the instability of all these movements. They pass in fact very quickly and very subtly from one to the other. We can erase the sign in the classical way of a philosophy of intuition and of presence. This philosophy erases the sign by making it derivative; it cancels reproduction and representation by turning them into a modification that supervenes over a simple presence. But since such a philosophy—and in truth it is *the* philosophy and history of the West—has in this way constituted and established the very concept of the sign, this concept, at the moment of its origin and in the heart of its sense, is marked by this will to derivation and erasure. Consequently, to restore the originality and the non-derivative character of the sign against classical metaphysics is also, by means of an apparent paradox, to erase the concept of the sign whose entire history and entire sense belong to the adventure of the metaphysics of presence. This schema holds as well for the concepts of representation, of repetition, of difference, etc., as well as for their entire system. The movement of this schema will only be able, for the moment and for a long time, to work over from within, from a certain inside, the language of metaphysics. This work undoubtedly has always already begun. We would have to grasp what happens in this inside when the closure of metaphysics comes to be named.

With the difference between real presence and presence in representation as *Vorstellung*, we find thus, by means of language, a whole system of differences drawn into the same deconstruction:[3] <58> the differences between the represented and the representative in general, the signified and the signifier, simple presence and its reproduction, presentation as *Vorstellung* and re-presentation as *Vergegenwärtigung*. This happens because re-presentation has a presentation (*Präsentation*) as *Vorstellung* for its represented. In this way—against Husserl's express intention—we come to make *Vorstellung* in general and, as such, depend on the possibility of repetition, and the most simple *Vorstellung*, presentation (*Gegenwärtigung*), depend on the possibility of re-presentation (*Vergegenwärtigung*). We derive the presence-of-the-present from repetition and not the reverse. This claim is against Husserl's express intention, but not without taking into account—as will perhaps appear later—what is discovered in his description of the movement of temporalization and of the relation to the other.

Naturally, the concept of *ideality* must be at the center of this kind of problematic. The structure of discourse can only be described, according to Husserl, as ideality. There is the ideality of the sensible form of the signifier (for example, the sensible form of the word) which must remain the *same* and can remain the same only insofar as it is an ideality.

Then there is the ideality of the signified (of the *Bedeutung*) or of the intended sense, which is to be confused neither with the act of intending nor with the object, since these last two cases might, as it may turn out, not be ideal. Finally, there is the ideality, in certain cases, of the object itself which then secures (this is what happens in the exact sciences) the ideal transparency and perfect univocity of language.*,4 But this ideality, which is only the name of the permanence of the same and the possibility of its repetition, does not *exist* in the world and it does not come from another world. It depends entirely on the possibility of acts of repetition. It is constituted by the possibility of acts of repetition. Its "being" is proportionate to the power of repetition. Absolute ideality is the correlate of a possibility of indefinite repetition. We can therefore say that being is determined by Husserl as ideality, that is, as repetition. Historical progress <59> always has for its essential form, according to Husserl, the constitution of idealities whose repetition, and therefore tradition, will be assured to infinity: repetition and tradition, that is, the transmission and reactivation of the origin. And this determination of being as ideality is really a *valuation,* an ethico-theoretical act which reawakens the originary decision of philosophy in its Platonic form. Husserl at times admits this; what he always opposes is a conventional Platonism. When he asserts the non-existence or the non-reality of ideality, he does this in order to acknowledge that ideality *is* according to a mode that is irreducible to sensible existence or to empirical reality, indeed, to their fiction.† By determining the *ontos on* as *eidos,* Plato was doing nothing else.

Now—and here once again we have to articulate the commentary on the interpretation—this determination of being as ideality is merged in a paradoxical way with the determination of being as presence. This is the case not only because pure ideality is always that of an ideal

---

* See on this subject "The Origin of Geometry," and §5 of the introduction to the French translation.

† The assertion implied by all of phenomenology is that of Being (*Sein*) as non-reality, non-existence, that of the *Ideal.* This pre-determination is the first word of phenomenology. Although it does not exist, ideality is nothing less than a non-being. Husserl says, "Each attempt to transform the being of what is ideal [*das Sein des Idealen*] into the possible being of what is real [*in ein mögliches Sein von Realem*] must obviously suffer shipwreck on the fact that possibilities themselves are ideal objects. Possibilities can as little be found in the real world as can numbers in general, or triangles in general" (*Logical Investigations,* Second Investigation, chapter 1, §4). <Translator: The equivalent passage can be found on page 243 of the English translation, volume 1.> Husserl also writes, "It is naturally not our intention to put *the being of what is ideal on a level with the thought-being of the fictitious or the absurd* [*Widersinnigen*]" (*Logical Investigations,* Second Investigation, chapter 1, §8). <Translator: The equivalent passage can be found on page 249 of the English translation, volume 1; these are Husserl's italics.>

"ob-ject," standing over and against, being pre-sent in front of, the act of repetition—*Vor-stellung* being the general form of presence as proximity to a look—but also because alone a temporality, determined on the basis of the living present as its source, determined on the basis of the now as "source-point," can secure the purity of ideality, that is, the openness of the repetition of the same to infinity. What does the "principle of all principles" <60> of phenomenology actually mean? What does the value of originary presence to intuition as the source of sense and evidence, as the *a priori* of *a priori,* mean? It means first the certainty, which is itself ideal and absolute, that the universal form of all experience (*Erlebnis*) and therefore of all life, has always been and always will be the *present.* There is and there will have never been anything but the present. Being is presence or the modification of presence. The relation to the presence of the present as the ultimate form of being and ideality is the movement by which I transgress empirical existence, factuality, contingency, mundanity, etc.—and first of all *mine.* To think presence as the universal form of transcendental life is to open me to the knowledge that in my absence, beyond my empirical existence, prior to my birth and after my death, *the present is.* I can empty it of all empirical content; I can imagine an absolute upheaval of the *content* of all possible experience, a radical transformation of the world. Doing this will not affect the universal form of presence about which I have a strange and unique certitude, since that form concerns no determinate being. It is therefore the relation to *my death* (to my disappearance in general) that is hidden in this determination of being as presence, ideality, as the absolute possibility of repetition. The possibility of the sign is this relation to death. The determination and the erasure of the sign in metaphysics is the dissimulation of this relation to death which nevertheless was producing signification.

If the possibility of my disappearance in general must be in a certain way experientially lived so that a relation to presence in general can be instituted, we can no longer say that the experience of the possibility of my absolute disappearance (of my death) comes to affect me, supervenes over an *I am* and modifies a subject. The *I am,* being experientially lived only as an *I am present,* presupposes in itself the relation to presence in general, to being as presence. The appearing of the *I* to itself in the *I am* is therefore originarily the relation to its own possible disappearance. *I am* means therefore originarily *I am* <61> *mortal. I am immortal* is an impossible proposition.* We can therefore go further. Insofar as it is

---

* Making use of the distinctions from the "pure logical grammar" and from *Formal and Transcendental Logic,* we have to specify this impossibility as follows. This proposition of course makes sense. It constitutes an intelligible discourse. It is not *sinnlos.* But within this

language, "I am the one who is" is the confession of a mortal. The movement that leads from the *I am* to the determination of my being as *res cogitans* (therefore as immortality) is the movement by which the origin of presence and of ideality snatches itself away within the presence and the ideality that it makes possible.

The erasure (or the derivation) of the sign is thereby merged with the reduction from imagination. Husserl's situation in regard to the tradition is ambiguous here. Undoubtedly, Husserl profoundly renews the problematic of imagination. And the role that he reserves for fiction in the phenomenological method indeed indicates that imagination is not in his eyes one faculty among many. Nevertheless, without neglecting the novelty and the rigor of the phenomenological descriptions of the image, we must notice the inheritance there. Although Husserl constantly emphasizes that, in contrast to memory, the image is a "neutralizing" and non-"positing" representation, that this characteristic gives it a privileged place in "phenomenological" practice, all this does not call into question the general concept under which the image is classified with memory: "representation" (*Vergegenwärtigung*), that is, the reproduction of a presence, even if what is produced is a pure fictional object of that presence. It follows that imagination is not a simple "neutralizing modification," even if it is neutralizing ("A very likely confusion must be guarded against, <62> namely the confusion between *neutrality-modification* and *imagination*").[5] It also follows that its neutralizing operation comes to modify a positing re-presentation (*Vergegenwärtigung*), namely, that of memory ("More precisely stated: universally *imagination* is the *neutrality modification* of '*positing*' *presentification*, therefore of memory in the widest conceivable sense").[6] Consequently, if it is a good auxiliary instrument for phenomenological neutralization, the image is not pure neutralization. It keeps within itself the primary reference to an originary presentation, that is, to a perception and to a positing of existence, to a belief in general.

This is why the pure ideality to which neutralization provides access is not fictional. This theme appears very early[*] and it will constantly fortify the polemic against Hume. But it is not by accident that Hume's thought more and more fascinated Husserl. The power of pure repetition that opens ideality and the power that liberates the imaginative

---

intelligibility, and for the reason that we just indicated, this proposition is "absurd" (with the absurdity of contradiction—*Widersinnigkeit*) and *a fortiori* "false." But since the classical idea of truth which guides these distinctions has itself issued from this way of getting rid of the relation to death, this "falseness" is the truth itself of truth. Therefore, it would be necessary to interpret these movements by means of other, wholly other "categories" (if we can still call such thoughts "categories").

[*] See in particular, the Second Logical Investigation, chapter 2.

reproduction of empirical perception cannot be foreign to one another. The same holds for what they produce.

Also, on more than one point, the First Logical Investigation is quite disconcerting in this regard.

1. First, it is disconcerting insofar as expressive phenomena in their expressive purity are considered representations of imagination (*Phantasievorstellungen*).

2. In the sphere of interiority which is thus opened by this fiction, we are calling the communicative discourse that a subject can contingently address to himself ("you have gone wrong") fictional. Calling it fictional allows one to think that a non-communicative, purely expressive discourse can *actually* take place in the "solitary life of the soul."

3. Thereby we assume that, in communication, where the same words, the same expressive kernels are at work, where <63> consequently pure idealities are indispensable, a rigorous distinction can be made between the fictional and the actual, and then between the ideal and the real, and that, consequently, actuality comes to be put on like an empirical piece of clothing that is external to expression, just like a body on a soul. And Husserl really makes use of these notions, even when he emphasizes the unity of the soul and the body in intentional *animation*. This unity does not undermine the essential distinction since it remains always a unity of composition.

4. Within the pure, internal "representivity," in the "solitary life of the soul," certain types of discourse could actually be held, as *actually* representative (this would be the case of expressive language and, let us say this already, purely objective, theoretico-logical discourse), while certain others are still purely *fictional* (these fictions located in the fiction would be the indicative acts of communication between myself and myself, myself as another and myself as myself, etc.).

If we admit, as we have tried to show, that every sign in general consists in an originarily repetitive structure, the general distinction between fictional usage and actual usage of a sign is threatened. *The sign is originarily worked over by fiction.* Therefore, whether we are dealing with indicative communication or expression, there is no sure criterion by means of which to distinguish between an external language and an internal language, and even if we grant the hypothesis of an internal language, there is no sure criterion for distinguishing between an actual language and a fictional language. Such a distinction, however, is indispensable for Husserl in order to prove that indication is external to expression, and for all that this distinction governs. If we declare that this distinction is illegitimate, we foresee a whole chain of formidable consequences for phenomenology.

What we just said about the sign holds thereby for the act of the speaking subject. Husserl was saying therefore that "in the genuine sense of communication, there is no speech in such cases, nor does one tell oneself anything: one merely represents [*man stellt sich vor*] oneself as speaking and communicating."[7] That statement <64> leads us to the *second argument* that Husserl announced. Husserl must assume therefore a difference between actual communication and the representation of the self as speaking subject such that the self-representation can come only to be joined onto the act of communication contingently and from the exterior. Now the originary structure of repetition that we just evoked in relation to the sign must govern the totality of the acts of signification. The subject cannot speak without giving to himself his representation, and that representation is not an accident. We can therefore no more imagine an actual discourse without self-representation than a representation of discourse without actual discourse. Undoubtedly this representivity can be modified, complicated, reflected according to the originary modes that the linguist, the semiologist, the psychologist, the theoretician of literature or art, even the philosopher will be able to study. These modes can be very original. But all of them presuppose the originary unity of discourse and the representation of discourse. Discourse represents itself, *is* its representation. Better, discourse is *the* self-representation.*

In a more general way, Husserl seems to admit that there can be a simple exteriority between the subject such as he is in his actual experience and what he represents to himself to be living. The subject would believe that he is saying something to himself and communicating something to himself; in truth he would do nothing of the kind. We might be tempted to conclude on this basis that, since consciousness is then entirely invaded by the belief or the illusion of speaking-to-himself, an entirely false consciousness, the truth of the experience would be of <65> the order of non-consciousness. It is the opposite: consciousness is the self-presence of the living, of the *Erleben*, of experience. The latter is simple and is never, essentially, affected by illusion since it relates only to

---

* But if the *re-* of this re-presentation does not say the simple duplication—repetitive or reflective—that *supervenes* over a simple presence (which is what the word "representation" has always *wanted to say*), then what we are approaching or advancing here concerning the relation between presence and representation must be opened up to other names. What we are describing as originary representation can be designated under this title only within the closure that we are attempting here to transgress, depositing in the closure, demonstrating in the closure contradictory or untenable propositions, attempting to produce securely insecurity in the closure, opening it up to its outside, which can be done only from a certain inside.

itself in an absolute proximity. The illusion of speaking-to-oneself would float on its surface as an empty, peripheral, and secondary consciousness. Language and its representation would come to be added to a simple consciousness simply present to itself, to a lived-experience, in any case, which can reflect in silence its own presence. As Husserl will say in *Ideas I*, "Each lived-experience in general (each lived-experience actually alive, if we can say that) is a lived-experience according to the mode of 'being present.' Belonging to its essence is the possibility of reflection on the same essence in which it is necessarily characterized as *being* certain and present."[8] The sign would be foreign to this self-presence, which is the foundation of presence in general. Because the sign is foreign to the self-present of the living present, we can say that it is foreign to presence in general, in what we believe to be able to recognize under the name of intuition or perception.

For—and this is the final argument in this section of the *Investigations*—if representation in indicative discourse is false, in monologue it is useless. If the subject indicates nothing to himself, this is because he cannot do it and he cannot indicate anything to himself because he has no need to do so. Since the lived-experience is immediately present to itself according to the mode of certainty and absolute necessity, the manifestation of the self to itself by means of delegation or the representation of an indexical is impossible because it is superfluous. It would be, in all senses of the word, *without reason*—therefore without cause. It would be without a cause because it would be without a purpose, "zwecklos," as Husserl says.

This *Zwecklosigkeit* of internal communication is the non-alterity, the non-difference in the identity of presence as self-presence. Of course, this concept of *presence* does not merely involve the enigma of the appearing of a being in absolute proximity to itself; it also designates the temporal essence of this <66> proximity, and this does not help to dispel the enigma. The self-presence of lived-experience has to be produced in the present as now. And this is really what Husserl says: if "psychical acts" are not announced by themselves through the intermediary of a "Kundgabe," if they are not to be informed about themselves through the intermediary of indications, this is because they are "experientially lived by us at that very instant [*im selben Augenblick*]."[9] The present of self-presence would be as indivisible as a *blink of an eye*.

5

The Sign and the Blink of an Eye

<67> The sharp point of the instant, the identity of lived-experience present to itself in the same instant bears therefore the whole weight of this demonstration. Self-presence must be produced in the undivided unity of a temporal present in order to have nothing to make known to itself by the proxy of the sign. Such a perception or intuition of the self by the self in presence would be not only the instance in which "signification" in general would not be able to have a place, it would also secure the possibility of an originary perception or intuition in general, that is, *non-signification* as the "principle of all principles." And later, each time that Husserl would like to indicate the sense of originary intuition, he will recall that originary intuition is the experience of the absence and uselessness of the sign.*

<68> The demonstration that concerns us occurs at a point in time earlier than *The Phenomenology of Internal Time-Consciousness*. And for systematic as well as historical reasons, the temporality of lived-experience is not a theme of the *Logical Investigations*. However, given the point where

---

* For example, the entire Sixth Logical Investigation constantly demonstrates that, between the acts and intuitive content on the one hand and the acts and the signifying contents on the other, the phenomenological difference is "irreducible." See especially §26. And yet the possibility of a "mixture" is admitted there, and this mixture would raise more than one question. The entire *Phenomenology of Internal Time-Consciousness* rests on the radical discontinuity between intuitive presentation and "the symbolic representation which not only represents the object in an empty way, but also the representation 'through' signs or images." <Translator: Throughout this chapter, Derrida cites Dussort's French translation of *The Phenomenology of Internal Time-Consciousness*. The equivalent passage for this citation can be found in appendix 2, on page 134.> In *Ideas I,* we can read, "Between *perception* on one side and *symbolic representation through image or sign* on the other, an unbridgeable eidetic difference exists. . . . We lapse into absurdity when we mix, as is done ordinarily, these modes of representation whose structures differ essentially, etc." *Ideas I,* §43. <Translator: The passage can be found on page 93 of the Kersten translation.> And what Husserl says about the perception of the sensible, corporeal thing is how he thinks of perception in general, namely, that, being given in person in its presence, the sensible, corporeal thing is a "sign for itself" (*Ideas I,* §52 <Translator: The passage can be found on page 121.>). Isn't it the case that being a sign of itself (*index sui*) is the same thing as not being a sign? In this sense, "at the very instant" it is perceived, the lived-experience is a sign of itself, present to itself without indicative detour.

we are in the *Logical Investigations,* we cannot avoid noting that a certain concept of the "now," of the present as the punctuality of the instant, authorizes discretely but in a decisive way the entire system of "essential distinctions." If the punctuality of the instant is a myth, a spatial or mechanical metaphor, a metaphysical concept inherited, or all of that at once, if the present of the presence to self is not *simple,* if it is constituted in an originary or irreducible synthesis, then the principle of Husserl's entire argumentation is threatened.

Here we cannot examine closely the admirable analyses found in *The Phenomenology of Internal Time-Consciousness,* analyses about which Heidegger says in *Sein und Zeit* that they are the first, in the history of philosophy, to break with a concept of time inherited from Aristotle's *Physics* and determined on the basis of the notions of "now," of "point," of "limit," and of "circle."[1] Let us, however, try to take from Husserl's analyses some points of reference for the viewpoint that we are occupying.

1. The concept of *punctuality,* of the *now,* of the *stigmē,* regardless of whether or not it is a metaphysical presupposition, still plays a role there that is major. Undoubtedly, no *now* can be isolated as an instant and pure punctuality. Not only does Husserl recognize it ("it belongs to the essence of lived-experiences that they must be spread out in this way, that lived-experience can never have in it an isolated punctual phase"),[2] <69> but his entire description is adapted, with an incomparable suppleness and perceptiveness, to the original modifications of this irreducible spreading-out. Nevertheless this spreading-out is still thought and described on the basis of the self-identity of the now as a point, as "source-point." The idea of originary presence and in general of "beginning," the "absolute beginning," the *principium,** always refers, in phenomenology, to this "source-point." Although the flowing of time is "indivisible into

---

* This is perhaps the right place to reread the definition of the "principle of all principles": "Enough of absurd theories. No conceivable theory can make us err with respect to the *principle of all principles:* that *every originary giving intuition is a legitimizing source [Rechtsquelle] of knowledge,* that everything that is offered to us in *"intuition" in an originary way* (so to speak in its corporeal reality) *must be simply received as what it gives itself out to be,* but *only within the limits in which it then gives itself.* Let our insight grasp this fact that the theory itself in its turn could not derive its truth except from originary givens. Every statement which does nothing more than give expression to such givens through merely unfolding their signification and adjusting it accurately is thus really, as I have put it in the introductory words of this chapter, an *absolute beginning,* called in a genuine sense to provide foundations, a *principium." Ideas I,* §24. <Translator: The equivalent passage can be found on page 44 of the Kersten translation. The italics are Husserl's.>

fragments that could be by themselves, and indivisible into phases that could be by themselves, into points of continuity," the "modes of the flowing of an immanent temporal object have a beginning, a, so to speak, source-point. This is the mode of flowing by which the immanent object begins to be. It is characterized as present."[3] Despite all the complexity of its structure, temporality has a non-displaceable center, an eye or a living nucleus, and that is the punctuality of the actual now. The "apprehension-of-the-now is as it were the nucleus of a comet's tail of retentions,"[4] and "there is each time but a present punctual phase that is now, while the others link themselves to it as a retentional tail."[5] "The actually present *now* is necessarily something punctual and remains something punctual [*ein Punktuelles*] <70>; it is a form that persists while the matter is always new."[6]

It is to this self-identity of the actual current now that Husserl is referring with the "im selben Augenblick," with which we started. Moreover, there is no possible objection, within philosophy, in regard to this privilege of the present-now. This privilege defines the very element of philosophical thought. It is *evidentness* itself, conscious thought itself. It governs every possible concept of truth and of sense. We cannot raise suspicions about it without beginning to enucleate consciousness itself from an elsewhere of philosophy which takes away from discourse all possible *security* and every possible *foundation*. And it is really around the privilege of the actual present, of the now, that, in the last analysis, this debate, which resembles no other, is played out between philosophy, which is always a philosophy of presence, and a thought of non-presence, which is not inevitably its opposite nor necessarily a meditation on negative absence, or even a theory of non-presence *as* unconscious.

The domination of the now is not only systematic with the founding opposition of metaphysics, namely, that of *form* (or *eidos* or idea) and *matter* as the opposition of *actuality* and *potentiality* ("The actually present now is necessarily and remains something punctual: it is a form that persists [*Verharrende*] while the matter is always new").[7] It secures the tradition that continues the Greek metaphysics of presence into the "modern" metaphysics of presence as self-consciousness, the metaphysics of the idea as representation (*Vorstellung*). It therefore prescribes the place of a problematic that puts phenomenology into confrontation with every thought of non-consciousness that would know how to approach the genuine stakes and profound agency where the decision is made: the concept of time. It is not by chance that *The Phenomenology of Internal Time-Consciousness* <71> confirms the domination of the present and rejects at once the "after-the-fact" way that an "unconscious content" becomes conscious, that is, the structure of temporality implied by all of Freud's texts.* In fact, Husserl writes,

> It is a genuine absurdity to speak of an "unconscious" content that becomes conscious after the fact [*nachträglich*]. Consciousness [*Bewußtsein*] is necessarily being-conscious [*bewußtsein*] in each of its phases. Just as the retentional phase is conscious of the preceding phase, without making it an object, what is originarily given is already conscious—and under the specific form of the "now"—without being objective. . . . The retention of an unconscious content is impossible. . . . If each "content" is in itself and necessarily "originarily conscious," it would be absurd to question one about a consciousness that would be given to it later.†

2. Despite this motive for the punctual now as the "archi-form" (*Ur-form*) (*Ideas I*) of consciousness, the content of the description in *The Phenomenology of Internal Time-Consciousness* and elsewhere forbids us from speaking of a simple self-identity of the present. We thereby find shaken not only what we could call the metaphysical security par excellence, but also, more locally, the argument of the "im selben Augenblick" found in the *Logical Investigations*.

---

* See on this subject our essay, "Freud and the Scene of Writing," in *Writing and Difference*. <Translator: The essay can be found on pages 196–231. The phrase "after-the-fact" renders "après-coup," which is the standard French translation of Freud's "Nachträglichkeit." In this essay, Derrida says, "Let us note in passing that the concepts of *Nachträglichkeit* and *Verspätung*, concepts which govern the whole of Freud's thought and determine all his other concepts, are already present and named in the *Project [for a Scientific Psychology]*" (p. 203). For a representative discussion of *Nachträglichkeit*, see *The Complete Psychological Works of Sigmund Freud, Volume XII (1911–1913), The Case of Schreber* (London: Hogarth, 1958), 67; here "Nachträglichkeit" is rendered as "after-pressure.">

† *The Phenomenology of Internal Time-Consciousness*, appendix 9. <Translator: The equivalent passage can be found on pages 162–63. Here Derrida seems to have misread Husserl's text. First, Husserl's text twice states "Bewußtsein" and not, as Derrida's translation implies, one time "Bewußtsein" (consciousness) and the second time "bewußtsein" (being-conscious). Churchill's English translation says, "Consciousness is necessarily consciousness in each of its phases." Then at the end of the citation Derrida seems to be using the Dussort translation of the original 1928 edition of Husserl's lectures on time-consciousness. The 1928 edition (edited by Heidegger) has "unbewußt" (see page 473); thus the Dussort French translation states "inconscient" (see page 161). The later Husserliana volume X (page 119) has "urbewußt," which is rendered by Brough as "primal consciousness"; see page 123 of *On the Phenomenology of the Consciousness of Internal Time* and note 18. Churchill's English translation, which is also based on the 1928 edition, states "unconscious." Here I have followed the corrected edition, which more clearly supports Derrida's interpretation. My thanks to Rudolf Bernet who pointed this mistake out to me.>

All of *The Phenomenology of Internal Time-Consciousness,* in its critical work as well as in its descriptive work, demonstrates and confirms of course the irreducibility of re-presentation (*Vergegenwärtigung, Repräsentation*) to presentational perception (*Gegenwärtigung, Präsentation*), the irreducibility of secondary and reproductive memory to retention, of imagination to originary impression, and of the reproduced now to the actual current now, whether it is perceived or retained, etc. Without being able to follow here the rigorous way in which *The Phenomenology of Internal Time-Consciousness* proceeds, and without it being <72> necessary thereby to question the demonstrative validity of its treatment, we can still question its evidentiary soil and the *milieu* of these distinctions, question them about what relates the terms distinguished to one another and constitutes the very possibility of the *comparison.*

We see very quickly then that the presence of the perceived present is able to appear as such only insofar as it is in *continuous composition* with a non-presence and a non-perception, namely, primary memory and primary anticipation (retention and protention). These non-perceptions are not added on, do not accompany *contingently* the actually perceived now; indispensably and essentially they participate in its possibility. No doubt Husserl says that retention is still a perception. But it is the absolutely unique case—Husserl has never spoken of another—of a perception whose perceived is not a present but a past as the modification of the present:

> If we call perception *the act in which every origin resides, the act that constitutes originarily,* then *primary memory* is *perception.* For *it is only in primary memory that we see the past,* it is only in it that the past is constituted, and this happens not in a re-presentational way but on the contrary in a presentational way.[8]

Thus, in retention, the presentation that gives us something to see delivers a non-present, a past and inactual present. We can therefore suspect that if Husserl nevertheless calls this perception, it is because he is holding on to the radical discontinuity as passing between retention and reproduction, between perception and imagination, etc., and not between perception and retention. This is the *nervus demonstrandi* of his criticism of Brentano. Husserl absolutely holds onto there being "absolutely no question of a continuous mediation of perception with its opposite."[9]

And yet, in the preceding section, was not the question of a continuous mediation posed in a really explicit way? Husserl says,

> If we now relate the term perception with *the differences in the way of being given* which temporal objects have, *the opposite of perception* is then

<73> *primary memory* and *primary anticipation* (retention and protention) which here comes on the scene, so that *perception* and *non-perception* pass *continuously* into one another.[10]

And later, he writes,

> In the ideal sense, perception (impression) would then be the phase of consciousness that constitutes the pure now, and memory, an entirely different phase of the continuity. But here we are only dealing precisely with an ideal limit, something abstract which can be nothing by itself. Nevertheless, even this ideal now is not something different *toto caelo* from the non-now, but on the contrary is in continuous commerce with it. And the continuous passage of perception into primary memory corresponds to that.[11]

As soon as we admit this continuity of the now and the non-now, of perception and non-perception in the zone of originarity that is common to originary impression and to retention, we welcome the other into the self-identity of the *Augenblick,* non-presence and non-evidentness into the *blink of an eye of the instant.* There is a duration to the blink of an eye and the duration closes the eye. This alterity is even the condition of presence, of presentation, and therefore of *Vorstellung* in general, prior to all the dissociations which could be produced there. The difference between retention and reproduction, between primary memory and secondary memory, is not the difference—not the radical difference that Husserl would want—between perception and non-perception, but between two modifications of non-perception. Whatever the phenomenological difference might be between these two modifications, despite the immense problems that the difference poses and the necessity of taking them into account, it separates only two ways of being related to the irreducible non-presence of another now. This relation to non-presence, once more, does not take by surprise, surround, or even dissimulate the presence of the originary impression; it allows its upsurge and its ever reborn virginity. But it radically destroys every possibility of self-identity in its simplicity. And that holds for the constituting flow itself at its greatest <74> depth:

> If we compare now the *constituting* phenomena to these constituted unities, we find a *flow,* and at each phase of this flow is a *continuity of shading.* But in principle it is impossible to display any phase of this flow in a continuous succession and therefore to transform in thought the flow to such an extent that this phase is extended into identity with itself.[12]

This intimacy of non-presence and alterity with presence cuts into, at its root, the argument for the uselessness of the sign in the self-relation.

    3. No doubt Husserl would refuse to assimilate the necessity of retention with the necessity of the sign, since the sign alone belongs, like the image, to the genus of re-presentation and symbol. And Husserl cannot renounce this rigorous distinction without putting the axiomatic *principium* of phenomenology in question. The vigor with which he supports the idea that retention and protention belong to the sphere of originarity provided that we understand it in a "broad sense," the insistence with which he opposes the absolute validity of primary memory to the relative validity of secondary memory,* these indeed manifest <75> his intention and uneasiness. He is uneasy because what is at issue is to save together two apparently irreconcilable possibilities: (a) the living now is constituted as the absolute perceptual source only in continuity with retention as non-perception. The faithfulness to experience and to "the things themselves" forbids that the source be constituted in any other way. (b) Since the source of certainty in general is the originarity of the living now, it is necessary to maintain retention in the sphere of originary certainty and shift the border between originarity and non-originarity

---

* See, for example, among many other analogous texts, appendix 3 to *The Phenomenology of Internal Time-Consciousness:* "We have therefore, as essential modes of the consciousness of time: 1) the 'sensation' as presentation, and retention and protention interwoven [*verflochtene*] essentially with it, but which can also become independent (the originary sphere in the large sense); 2) thetic re-presentation (memory), thetic re-presentation of what can accompany or return (anticipation); 3) imaginary re-presentation, as pure imagination, in which we discover all these same modes, in a consciousness that imagines." <The equivalent passage can be found on page 142 of *The Phenomenology of Internal Time-Consciousness.*> Here again, as we have noticed, the nucleus of the problem has the form of the interweaving (*Verflechtung*) of threads, which phenomenology painstakingly unravels in their essence.

    This extension of the sphere of originarity is what allows us to distinguish between the absolute certainty attached to retention and the relative certainty dependent on secondary memory and recollection (*Wiedererinnerung*) in the form of re-presentation. Speaking of perceptions as archi-lived-experiences (*Urerlebnisse*), Husserl writes in *Ideas I:* "They have in their concretion, more precisely considered, only *one*, but also always a continuously flowing, *absolutely originary* phase—the moment of the living *now.*" He goes on, "Thus, for example, we seize upon *the absolute validity* of reflection *insofar as* it is immanent *perception,* that is, pure and simple immanent perception, and more particularly, with respect to what, in its flowing away, it actually makes given originarily; similarly, the *absolute validity of retention of something immanent* with respect to what is intended in it in the characteristic of what is 'still' living and what has 'just now' been, but of course only so far as the content of what is thus characterized reaches. . . . We likewise seize upon the *relative* validity of recollection of something immanent" (*Ideas I,* §78). <Translator: The equivalent passages can be found on pages 180–81 of the Kersten translation. The emphasis is Husserl's.>

so that it passes, not between the pure present and the non-present, between the actuality and the non-actuality of a living now, but between two forms of re-turn or of the re-stitution of the present, re-tention and re-presentation.

Without reducing the abyss that can in fact separate retention from re-presentation, without concealing that the problem of their relations is nothing other than the history of "life" and of life's becoming-conscious, we must be able to say *a priori* that their common root, the possibility of re-petition in its most general form, the trace in the most universal sense, is a possibility that not only must inhabit the pure actuality of the now, but also must constitute it by means of the very movement of the différance that the possibility inserts into the pure actuality of the now.[13] Such a trace is, if we are able to hold onto this language without contradicting it and erasing it immediately, more "originary" than the phenomenological originarity itself. The ideality of the form (*Form*) of presence itself implies consequently that it can be repeated to infinity, that its return, as the return of the same, is to infinity necessary and inscribed in <76> presence as such; that the re-turn is the return of a present that will be retained in a *finite* movement of retention; that there is originary truth, in the phenomenological sense, only insofar as it is enrooted in the finitude of this retention; finally that the relation to infinity can be instituted only in the openness to the ideality of the form of presence as the possibility of a re-turn to infinity. Without this non-identity to oneself of so-called originary presence, how are we to explain that the possibility of reflection and of re-presentation belongs to the essence of every lived-experience? How are we to explain that reflection belongs as an ideal and pure freedom to the essence of consciousness? Husserl constantly emphasizes this for reflection in *Ideas I,*[*] and for re-presentation already in *The Phenomenology of Internal Time-Consciousness.*[†] In all of these directions, the presence of the present is thought beginning from the fold of the return, beginning from the movement of repetition and not the reverse. Does not the fact that this fold in presence or in self-presence is irreducible, that this trace or this différance is always older than presence and obtains for it its openness, forbid us from speaking of a simple self-identity "im selben Augenblick"? Does not this fact compromise the use

---

* In particular, see §77, where he raises the problem of the difference and of the relations between reflection and re-presentation, for example, in secondary memory.
† See, for example, §42: "But the ideal possibility of an exactly matching re-presentation *of* this consciousness corresponds to every present and presenting consciousness." <Translator: The equivalent passage can be found on page 115 of *The Phenomenology of Internal Time-Consciousness.*>

Husserl wants to make of the "solitary life of the soul" and consequently the rigorous distribution between indication and expression? Is it not the case that indication and all the concepts from which we have attempted so far to think it (existence, nature, mediation, empiricity, etc.) have in the movement of transcendental temporalization an origin that cannot be uprooted? Likewise, is it not the case that all of what is announced in this reduction to the "solitary life of the soul" (the transcendental reduction in all of its stages and notably the reduction to the monodological sphere of the *"proper"—Eigenheit—*etc.) is not, as it were, fissured <77> in its possibility by what is called time? It is fissured by what has been called time and to which it would be necessary to give another title, since "time" has always designated a movement thought beginning from the present and since "time" can say nothing but the present. Must we not say that the concept of pure solitude—and of the monad in the phenomeno-logical sense—is *split open* by its own origin, by the very condition of its self-presence: "time" rethought beginning from the différance in auto-affection, beginning from the identity of identity and non-identity in the "same" of the *im selben Augenblick*? Husserl has himself evoked the analogy between the relation to the alter ego such that it is constituted within the absolute monad of the ego and the relation to the other (past) present such that it is constituted in the absolute actuality of the living present (*Cartesian Meditations,* §52). Is it not the case that this "dialectic"—in all the senses of this word and prior to every speculative resumption of this concept—opens living to différance, constituting in the pure immanence of lived-experience the *hiatus* of indicative communication and even of signification in general? We are indeed saying the hiatus of indicative communication *and of signification in general.* For Husserl intends not only to exclude indication from the "solitary life of the soul." He will consider language in general, the element of the *logos,* in its expressive form itself, as a secondary event, and added on to an originary and pre-expressive stratum of sense. Expressive language itself would have to supervene on the absolute silence of the self-relation.

The Voice That Keeps Silent

<78> Phenomenological "silence" can therefore be reconstituted only by a double exclusion or a double reduction: that of the relation to the other in me in indicative communication, and that of expression as a later stratum, superior to and external to the stratum of sense. The agency of the voice will make its strange authority be heard in the relation between these two exclusions.

Let us at the outset consider the first reduction, in the form in which it is announced in the "essential distinctions," to which we have taken as a rule to hold ourselves here. Indeed, it is necessary to recognize that the criterion of the distinction between expression and indication is in the end entrusted to an all too summary description of "interior life": in this interior life, there would be no indication because there is no communication; and there is no communication because there is no *alter ego*. And when the second person arises in interior language, it is a fiction, and fiction is only fiction. "You have gone wrong, you can't go on like that" is only a false communication, a pretending.

Let us not formulate *from the exterior* the questions which impose themselves upon the possibility and the status of such pretendings or fictions, or upon the place from which this "you" in the monologue may arise. Let us not pose these questions *yet*. Their necessity will be still more keen when Husserl will indeed have to note that, besides the "you," the personal pronoun in general and singularly the "I" are expressions that are "essentially occasional," deprived of "objective sense," and functioning always <79> as indexicals in actual discourse. The "I" alone achieves its meaning <*vouloir-dire*> in solitary discourse and functions outside of solitary discourse as a "universally operative indexical."[1]

For the moment, let us ask in what sense and in view of what the structure of interior life is here "simplified" and in what way the choice of examples is revelatory of Husserl's project. It is revelatory at least in two features.

1. These examples are of the *practical* order. In the propositions chosen, the subject addresses himself to himself as to a second person that he blames, exhorts, invites to a decision or to a regret. That proves, of course, that we are not dealing here with "indications." Nothing is shown, directly or indirectly. The subject learns nothing about himself.

His language refers to nothing that "exists." The subject is not informed about himself; neither *Kundgabe* nor *Kundnahme* are functioning. Husserl needs to choose his examples within the practical sphere in order to show at once that in them nothing is "indicated" and that these consist of false discourses. In fact, we might be tempted to conclude from these examples, by supposing that we are unable to find another genus of them, that interior discourse is always essentially practical, axiological, or axiopoetic. Even when one says to oneself "you are this way," is it not the case that the predication involves a valorizing or productive act? But it is precisely this temptation that Husserl wants above all and at all costs to avoid. He has always determined the model of language *in general*—indicative as well as expressive—by starting in the *theorein*. Whatever care he subsequently took to respect the originality of the practical stratum of sense and expression, whatever then has been the success and rigor of his analyses, Husserl never stopped asserting the reducibility of the axiological to its logico-theoretical nucleus.* ,2 <80> We rediscover here the necessity that drove him to study language from a logical and epistemological viewpoint, pure grammar as pure *logical* grammar that is governed more or less immediately by the possibility of a relation to the object. A false discourse is a discourse, a contradictory discourse (*widersinnig*) escapes from non-sense (*Unsinnigkeit*), only if its grammaticality does not forbid a meaning or an intention-of-*Bedeutung*, which itself can be determined only as the aim of an object.

Therefore we must notice that theoretical logicity, the *theorein* in general, governs not only the determination of expression, of logical signification, but also already what is excluded from it, namely, indication, monstration as *Weisen* or *Zeigen* in the *Hinweis* or the *Anzeigen*. And it is remarkable *that Husserl must, at a certain depth, have recourse to an essential theoretical nucleus of indication in order to be able to exclude it from an expressivity that is itself purely theoretical.* Perhaps, at this depth, the determination of expression is contaminated by the very thing that it excludes: pointing the finger at what is in front of one's eyes or at what must always be able to appear to an intuition in its visibility, the *Zeigen*—the relation to the object as indicative monstration—*is invisible only provisionally.* The *Zeigen* is always an intention (*Meinen*) which pre-determines the profound essential unity between the *Anzeigen* of indication and the *Hinzeigen* of expression. And the sign (*Zeichen*) would always refer, in the last analysis,

---

* See notably chapter 4 and especially §114 to 127 of *Ideas I* (part 3). We will study them elsewhere more closely and on their own. See "Form and Meaning," which has already been cited.

to *Zeigen,* to the space, to the visibility, to the field and horizon of what is ob-jected and pro-jected, to phenomenality as vis-à-vis and surface, evidentness or intuition, and first of all as light.

What, then, of the voice and time? If monstration is the unity of gesture and perception in the sign, if signification is attributed to the finger and to the eye, and if this attribution is prescribed to every sign, whether it is indicative or expressive, discursive or non-discursive, what do the voice and time have to do with it? If the invisible is the pro-visional, what do the voice and time have to do with it? And why does Husserl make such an effort <81> to separate indication and expression? Does pronouncing or hearing a sign reduce indicative spatiality or indicative mediacy? Let us be patient a bit longer.

2. The example chosen by Husserl ("you have gone wrong, you can't go on like that") must therefore prove two things at once. It must prove on the one hand that this proposition is not indicative (and therefore that it is a fictional communication); on the other that it provides no knowledge of the subject to himself. Paradoxically, the proposition is not indicative because, insofar as it is non-theoretical, non-logical, and non-cognitive, it is as well not expressive. This is why it would be a perfectly fictional phenomenon of signification. Thereby the unity of the *Zeigen* prior to its diffraction into indication and expression is verified. Now, the *temporal modality* of these propositions is not a matter of indifference. If these propositions are not propositions of knowledge, this is because they are not immediately in the form of predication. They do not utilize immediately the verb "to be," and their sense, if not their grammatical form, is not in the present. They take note of a past in the form of a reproach, an exhortation to regret something and to make amends. *The present indicative of the verb "to be"* is the pure, teleological form of the logicity of expression; or, better, it is the present indicative of the verb *to be* in the *third person.* Even more, it is the type of proposition, "S is P," in which the S is not a person for which we can replace a personal pronoun, the latter having in all real discourse a value that is solely indicative.* The subject S must be a name and a name of an object.

---

* See the First Logical Investigation, chapter 3, §26: "Every expression, in fact, that includes a *personal pronoun* lacks an objective sense. The word 'I' names a different person from case to case. . . . In its case, rather, an indicative function mediates and, so to speak, warns the hearer that the one who is in front of you aims at himself." <Translator: The equivalent passage can be found on pages 218–19 of the English translation, volume 1. Here, Derrida indicates that he is using the French translation with a "tr. fr."> The whole problem consists in knowing whether in solitary discourse, where, as Husserl says, the *Bedeutung* of the "I" is fulfilled and accomplished, the element of universality proper to expressivity as such does

And we <82> know that for Husserl "S is P" is the fundamental and primitive form, the originary apophantic operation from which every logical proposition must be able to be derived by simple complication.*,3 If one posits the identity of expression and logical *Bedeutung* (*Ideas I*, §124), one must therefore acknowledge that the third "person" of the present indicative of the verb "to be" is the irreducible and pure kernel of expression. Husserl was saying, we recall, about an expression, that it was not primitively an "expressing itself," but from the very beginning it is an "expressing itself about something" (*über etwas sich auszern*, see §7). The "speaking to oneself" that here Husserl wants to restore is not a "speaking-about-oneself-to-oneself," unless the latter can take the form of a "speaking to oneself that S is P."

It is here that one must *speak*. The sense of the verb "to be" (about which Heidegger tells us that its infinitive form has been enigmatically determined by philosophy on the basis of the third person of the present indicative)[4] entertains with the *word*, that is, with the unity of the *phonē* and sense, a relation that is entirely singular. Undoubtedly it is not a "simple word," since we can translate it into different languages. But as well it is not a conceptual generality.† Since, however, <83> its sense designates nothing, no thing, no being nor any ontic determination, since

---

not forbid this fulfillment and dispossesses the subject of the full intuition of the *Bedeutung* "I." As well, we have to know if solitary discourse interrupts or merely *interiorizes* the situation of dialogue in which, as Husserl says, "since each person, while speaking of himself, says 'I,' the word has the character of a universally operative indexical of this situation." <Translator: The equivalent passage can be found on page 219 of the English translation, volume 1.>

Thus we understand better the difference between the *manifested* which is always subjective and the *expressed* as named. Each time that the "I" appears, what is at issue is a proposition of indicative manifestation. The manifested and the named can at times partially overlap ("a glass of water, please" names the thing and manifests the desire), but the two are in principle perfectly disjunctive, as in the following example where they are perfectly disjunctive: $2 \times 2 = 4$. "This statement does not say what is said by 'I judge that $2 \times 2 = 4$.' They are not even equivalent statements, since the one can be true when the other is false" (First Logical Investigation, §25). <Translator: The equivalent passage can be found on page 313.>

*See, in particular, *Formal and Transcendental Logic*, part 1, chapter 1, §13.

† Whether we demonstrate this in the Aristotelian way or in the Heideggerian way, the sense of being must precede the general concept of being. Concerning the singularity of the relation between the word and the sense of being, as well as for the problem of the present indicative, we refer to *Sein und Zeit* and to *Introduction to Metaphysics*. Perhaps it already seems that, while finding support at decisive points in Heidegger's motives, we would like to wonder whether, in regard to the relations between *logos* and *phonē* and the claimed irreducibility of certain unities of words (of the word "being" or other "radical words"), Heidegger's thought at times calls forth the same questions as the metaphysics of presence.

we encounter it nowhere outside of the word, its irreducibility is that of the *verbum* or of the *legein,* that of the unity of thought and voice in the *logos.* The privilege of being cannot resist the deconstruction of the word. "Being" is the first or the last word to resist the deconstruction of a language of words. But why is verbality merged with the determination of being in general as presence? And why the privilege of the present indicative? Why is the epoch of the *phonē* the epoch of being in the form of presence, that is, in the form of ideality?

It is here that one must *hear oneself.* Let us return to Husserl. Pure expression, logical expression, must be for him an "unproductive" "medium" that happens to "reflect" (*widerzuspiegeln*) the stratum of pre-expressive sense.[5] Its sole productivity consists in making the sense pass into the ideality of the conceptual and universal form.[*] Although there are essential reasons why the sense is not completely repeated in the expression and why the expression involves dependent and incomplete significations (syncategoremes, etc.), the *telos* of complete expression is the restoration, in the form of presence, of the totality of a sense actually given to intuition. Since the sense is determined on the basis of a relation to the object, the medium of expression must protect, respect, and restore the *presence* of the sense, *at once as the being-in-front of the object* available to a look, and *as the proximity to oneself in interiority.* The *pre* of the *present ob*ject now-in-front-of is an *against* (*Gegen*wart, *Gegen*stand) at once <84> in the sense of the *up-against* of proximity and the *over-against* of the op-posite.

Now between idealization and the voice, the complicity is here unfailing. An ideal object is an object whose monstration can be indefinitely repeated, whose presence in the *Zeigen* is indefinitely reiterable precisely because, freed from all mundane spatiality, it is a pure noema which I can express without having, at least in appearance, to pass through the world. In this sense, the phenomenological voice, which seems to achieve this operation "in time," does not break with the order of *Zeigen;* it belongs to the same system and brings its function to completion. The passage to infinity in the idealization of the object is unified with the historial advent of the *phonē.*[6] This does not mean that we are able finally to understand what the movement of idealization is on the basis of a determinate "function" or "faculty," concerning which we could know what it *is,* thanks to the familiarity of experience, the "phenomenology of one's own body," or an objective science (phonetics, phonology, or physiology of phona-

---

[*] *Ideen I,* §124. <Translator: Here Derrida uses the German title, but perhaps it is a typographical error.>

tion). On the contrary. That the history of idealization, that is, the "history of spirit," or history as such, is inseparable from the history of the *phonē*, this inseparability restores to the *phonē* its enigmatic potency.

In order to really understand that in which the power of the voice resides, and that in which metaphysics, philosophy, the determination of being as presence are the epoch of the voice as the *technical* mastery of object-being, in order to really understand the unity of *technē* and *phonē*, it is necessary to think the objectivity of the object. The ideal object is the most objective of objects; it is independent of the *hic et nunc* of events and of the acts of the empirical subjectivity who intends it. The ideal object can be repeated, to infinity, while remaining the same. Its presence to intuition, its being-in-front-of for the look depends essentially on no mundane or empirical synthesis; the restoration of its sense in the form of presence becomes a universal and unlimited possibility. But its ideal-being is *nothing* outside of the world; it must be constituted, repeated, <85> and expressed in a medium that does not impair the presence and the self-presence of the acts that intend it: a medium that preserves at once the *presence of the object* in front of the intuition and the *presence to oneself*, the absolute proximity of the acts to themselves. Since the ideality of the object is only its being-for a non-empirical consciousness, it can be expressed only in an element whose phenomenality does not have the form of mundanity. *The voice is the name of this element. The voice hears itself.* Phonic signs ("acoustic images" in Saussure's sense, the phenomenological voice) are "heard" by the subject who utters them in the absolute proximity of their present. The subject does not have to pass outside of himself in order to be immediately affected by its activity of expression. My words are "alive" because they seem not to leave me, seem not to fall outside of me, outside of my breath, into a visible distance; they do not stop belonging to me, to be at my disposal, "without anything accessory." In any case, in this way, the phenomenon of the voice, the phenomenological voice, is *given*. Someone will object perhaps that this interiority belongs to the phenomenological and ideal side of every signifier. For example, the ideal form of a written signifier is not in the world, and the distinction between grapheme and the empirical body of the corresponding graphic sign separates an inside of phenomenological consciousness and an outside of the world. And that is true of every visible or spatial signifier. Of course. Nevertheless every non-phonetic signifier involves, right within its "phenomenon," within the (non-mundane) phenomenological sphere of experience in which it is given, a spatial reference; the sense of "outside," "in the world" is an essential component of its phenomenon. In appearance, there is nothing like that in the phenomenon of the voice. Within phenomenological interiority, hearing oneself and seeing oneself are two orders of the self-relation that are radically different. Even before a description of this difference is sketched, we understand why the hypothesis of the "monologue" could authorize the distinction between indication and expression only by assuming an essential connection between expression and the <86> *phonē*. Between the phonic element (in the phenomenological sense and not in the sense of intra-mundane sonority) and expressivity, that is, the logicity of a signifier *animated* in view of the ideal presence of a *Bedeutung* (which is itself related to an object), there would be a necessary connection. Husserl cannot bracket what the glossematicians call the "substance of expression" without threatening his entire project.[7] The appeal to this substance plays therefore a major philosophical role.

Let us therefore attempt to interrogate the phenomenological value of the voice, the transcendence of its dignity in relation to every other signifying substance. We think and we are trying to show that this transcendence is only apparent. But this "appearance" is the very essence of consciousness and its history, and it determines an epoch to which the philosophical idea of truth, the opposition of truth and appearance, such as it still functions in phenomenology, belongs. We can therefore neither call it "appearance" nor name it within metaphysical conceptuality. We cannot attempt to deconstruct this transcendence without plunging in, and groping our way through inherited concepts, toward the unnameable.

The "apparent transcendence" of the voice, therefore, is based on the fact that the signified, which is always essentially ideal, the "expressed" *Bedeutung,* is immediately present to the act of expression. This immediate presence is based on the fact that the phenomenological "body" of the signifier seems to erase itself in the very moment it is produced. From this point on, it seems to belong to the element of ideality. It reduces itself phenomenologically and transforms the mundane opacity of its body into pure diaphaneity. This erasure of the sensible body and of its exteriority is *for consciousness* the very form of the immediate presence of the signified.

Why is the phoneme the most "ideal" of signs? Where does this complicity between sound and ideality, or rather between voice and ideality, come from? (Hegel had been more attentive to this complicity than anyone else; and from the viewpoint <87> of the history of metaphysics, this is a remarkable fact that we shall interrogate elsewhere).[8] When I speak, it belongs to the phenomenological essence of this operation that *I hear myself during the time* that I speak. The signifier that is animated by my breath and by the intention of signification (in Husserlian language the expression animated by the *Bedeutungsintention*) is absolutely close to me. The living act, the act that gives life, the *Lebendigkeit* that animates the body of the signifier and transforms it into an expression that wants to say, the soul of language, seems not to separate itself from itself, from its presence to itself. The soul of language does not risk death in the body of a signifier abandoned to the world and to the visibility of space. The soul can *show* the ideal object or the ideal *Bedeutung*, which relates to it, without venturing outside of ideality, outside of the interiority of life present to itself. The system of *Zeigen*, the movements of the finger and the eye (about which we were wondering earlier if those movements were not inseparable from phenomenality) are not absent here; they are internalized. The phenomenon does not stop being an object for the voice. On the contrary, insofar as the ideality of the object seems to depend on the voice and thus becomes *absolutely available* in it, the system that connects phenomenality to the possibility of *Zeigen* functions better than ever in the voice. *The phoneme gives itself as the mastered ideality of the phenomenon.*

This presence to itself of the animating act in the transparent spirituality of what it animates, this intimacy of life to itself, which has always led us to say that speech is alive, all of this assumes therefore that the speaking subject hears himself in the present. Such is the essence or the normalcy of speech. It is implied in the very structure of speech that the speaker *hear himself*: that he at once perceive the sensible form of the phonemes and understand his own intention of expression. If accidents arise, which seem to contradict this teleological necessity, either they are surmounted by some supplementing operation or there will be no speech. Being dumb and being deaf go together. The deaf can participate in colloquy only by slipping <88> his actions into the form of words whose *telos* entails that they are heard by the one who utters them.

Considered from a purely phenomenological viewpoint, within the reduction, the process of speech has the originality of being already delivered as a pure phenomenon, having already suspended the natural attitude and the existential thesis of the world. The operation of "hearing-oneself-speak" is an auto-affection of an absolutely unique type. On the one hand, it operates in the medium of universality. The signifieds which appear in it must be idealities that we must *idealiter* be able to repeat or transmit indefinitely as the same. On the other hand, the subject is able to hear himself or speak to himself, is able to let himself be affected by the signifier that he produces without any detour through the agency of exteriority, of the world, or of the non-proper in general. Every other form of auto-affection must either pass through the non-proper or renounce universality. When I see myself, regardless of whether it occurs because a limited area of my body is given to my look or it occurs by means of a specular reflection, the non-proper is already there in the field of this auto-affection which thereafter is no longer pure. It is the same thing in the experience of touching-touched. In the two cases, the surface of my body, as a relation to exteriority, must begin by exposing itself in the world. Are there not, someone will say, forms of pure auto-affection which, in the interiority of one's own body, do not require the intervention of any mundane exhibitive surface and yet are not of the order of the voice? But then these forms remain purely empirical; they cannot belong to a medium of universal signification. It is necessary therefore, in order to give an account of the phenomenological power of the voice, to specify this concept of pure auto-affection and describe what in it makes it proper to universality. Insofar as it is pure auto-affection, the operation of hearing-oneself-speak seems to reduce even the internal surface of one's own body. In its phenomenon, it seems to be able to do without this exteriority within interiority, to do without this internal space in which our experience <89> or our image of one's own body is stretched out. This is why hearing-oneself-speak is lived as absolutely pure auto-affection, in a proximity to self which would be nothing other than the absolute reduction of space in general. It is this purity that makes it apt for universality. Requiring the intervention of no determinate surface in the world, *producing itself in the world as an auto-affection* that is pure, it is an absolutely available signifying substance. For the voice encounters no obstacle to its emission in the world precisely insofar as it produces itself there *as pure auto-affection.* Undoubtedly this auto-affection is the possibility of what we call *subjectivity* or the *for-itself,* but without it no world would appear *as such.* For, in its depth, the voice assumes the unity of the sound (which is in the world) and the *phonē* (in the phenomenological sense). An objective "mundane" science can surely teach us nothing about the essence of the voice. But the unity of the sound and the voice, which allows the voice to produce itself in the world as pure auto-affection, is the unique instance that escapes from the distinction between intramundanity and transcendentality; and by the same token, it makes this distinction possible.

It is this universality that results in the fact that, structurally and in principle, no consciousness is possible without the voice. The voice is being close to itself in the form of universality, as con-sciousness. The voice *is* consciousness. In colloquy, the propagation of signifiers seems to encounter no obstacle because it puts two *phenomenological* origins of pure auto-affection in relation. To speak to someone is undoubtedly to hear oneself speak, to be heard by oneself, but also and by the same token, if one is heard by the other, it is to make the other *repeat immediately* in himself the hearing-oneself-speak in the very form in which I have produced it. Repeat it immediately, that is, reproduce the pure auto-affection without the aid of any exteriority. This possibility of reproduction, whose structure is absolutely unique, *gives itself* as the phenomenon of an unlimited mastery or an unlimited power over the signifier, since the latter has the form of <90> non-exteriority itself. Ideally in the teleological essence of speech, it would therefore be possible that the signifier be absolutely near to the signified intended by intuition and guiding the meaning. The signifier would become perfectly diaphanous by reason of the absolute proximity of the signified. This proximity is broken, however, when, instead of hearing myself speak, I see myself write or signify by gestures.

Husserl will be able to consider the medium of expression as "unproductive" and "reflective" precisely on the condition of this absolute proximity of the signifier to the signified, and on the condition of the signifier's erasure in immediate presence. Also, on this condition, Husserl will be able, paradoxically, to reduce the medium with no harm being done and assert that a pre-expressive stratum of sense exists. On this condition too Husserl will give himself the right to reduce the totality of language, regardless of whether it is indicative or expressive, in order to regain the possession of the originarity of sense.

How are we to understand this reduction of language in light of the fact that Husserl, from the *Logical Investigations* up to "The Origin of Geometry," continues to consider there to be scientific truths, that is, absolutely ideal objects, only in "statements"? How are we to understand this reduction when he continued to think of not only spoken language but also *inscription* as indispensable for the constitution of ideal objects, that is, of objects that can be transmitted and repeated as the same?

First of all, one needs to recognize this: although the movement that results in "The Origin of Geometry" was started long before, in its most obvious aspect it confirms the profound way in which language is limited to a secondary stratum of experience, and, in the consideration of this secondary stratum, it confirms the traditional phonologism of metaphysics. If writing completes the constitution of ideal objects, it does this only insofar as it is phonetic writing.* Writing comes to stabilize, inscribe, <91> write down, incarnate a speech that is already prepared. And to reactivate writing is always to reawaken an expression within an indication, a word in the body of a letter which was carrying in it the threat of

---

* It is strange that, despite the formalist motif and the Leibnizian fidelity that he asserts from one end of his work to the other, Husserl has never placed the problem of writing at the center of his reflections, nor does he, in "The Origin of Geometry," take account of the difference between phonetic writing and non-phonetic writing.

the crisis, insofar as the letter was a symbol that can always remain empty. Speech was already playing the same role in regard to the identity of sense such as it is first constituted in thought. For example, the "proto-geometer".must produce in thought, by means of a passage to the limit, the pure ideality of the geometrical object, by securing its transmissibility by speech and then entrusting it to a writing by means of which someone will be able to repeat the originative sense, that is, the act of *pure thought* which created the ideality of the sense. With the possibility of progress that such an incarnation authorizes, the risk of "forgetfulness" and of loss of the sense grows constantly. It is more and more difficult to reconstitute the presence of the act that is buried under historical sedimentations. The moment of the crisis is always that of the sign. Moreover, despite the meticulousness, the rigor, and the absolute novelty of his analyses, Husserl always describes all of these movements in metaphysical concep-tuality. The absolute difference between the soul and the body is what governs. Writing is a body that expresses only if we actually pronounce the verbal expression that animates it, if its space is temporalized. The word is a body that means something only if an actual intention animates it and makes it pass from the state of inert sonority (*Körper*) to the state of animated body (*Leib*). This body proper of the word expresses only if it is animated (*sinnbelebt*) by the act of a wanting-to-say (*bedeuten*) which transforms it into spiritual flesh (*geistige Leiblichkeit*). But only *Geistigkeit* or *Leiblichkeit* is independent and originary.*,9 As such, *Geistigkeit* needs no signifier in order to be present to itself. It is as much against its signifiers as thanks to them that *Geistigkeit* is awakened and maintained in life. Such is the traditional side of Husserl's discourse.

<92> But if Husserl had to acknowledge, even as salutary threats, the necessity of these "incarnations," this is because a profound motive was tormenting and contesting, from within, the security of these tradi-tional distinctions. Because too the possibility of writing was inhabiting the inside of speech which itself was at work in the intimacy of thought.

And here we return to all the resources of originary non-presence whose outcrop we have already located several times. Even though he represses difference by pushing it back into the exteriority of the signi-fier, Husserl could not fail to recognize its work at the origin of sense and of presence. Auto-affection as the operation of the voice assumed that a pure difference came to divide self-presence. The possibility of everything that we believe we are able to exclude from auto-affection is enrooted in this pure difference: space, the outside, the world, the body, etc. As soon

---

* See the introduction to "The Origin of Geometry," §7.

as we admit that auto-affection is the condition of self-presence, no pure transcendental reduction is possible. But it is necessary to pass through the reduction in order to recapture the difference in closest proximity to itself: not to its identity, nor its purity, nor its origin. It has none of these. But in closest proximity to the movement of différance.

This movement of différance does not supervene upon a transcendental subject. The movement of différance produces the transcendental subject. Auto-affection is not a modality of experience that characterizes a being that would already be itself (*autos*). Auto-affection produces the same as the self-relation in the difference with itself, the same as the non-identical.

Shall we say that the auto-affection about which we have been speaking so far concerns only the operation of the voice, that the difference concerns the order of the phonic "signifier" or the "secondary stratum" of expression? Shall we say that we can always reserve the possibility of a pure and purely self-present identity at the level that Husserl wanted to open up, the level of pre-expressive lived-experience, the level of sense insofar as it preceded *Bedeutung* and expression?

<93> But it would be easy to show that such a possibility is excluded at the very root of transcendental experience.

In fact, why is the concept of auto-affection imposed on us? The originality of speech, that by which speech is distinguished from every other milieu of signification, comes from the way its fabric seems to be purely temporal. And this temporality does not unfold a sense that would be itself timeless. Even prior to being expressed, the sense is through and through temporal. The omnitemporality of ideal objects, according to Husserl, is only a mode of temporality. And when Husserl describes a sense that seems to escape from temporality, he hastens to specify that what is at issue in it is a provisional stage of the analysis and that he is considering a constituted temporality. Now as soon as we take account of the movement of temporalization, such as it is already described in *The Phenomenology of Internal Time-Consciousness,* it is indeed necessary to use the concept of pure auto-affection, the concept that Heidegger uses, as we know, in *Kant and the Problem of Metaphysics* precisely in regard to time.[10] The "source-point," the "originary impression," that on the basis of which the movement of temporalization is produced is already pure auto-affection. First, it is a pure production since temporality is never a real predicate of a being. The intuition of time itself cannot be empirical. It is a reception that receives nothing. The absolute novelty of each now is therefore engendered by nothing. It consists in an originary impression that engenders itself: "The originary impression is the absolute beginning of this production, the originary source, that starting from which all the rest is continuously produced. But it itself is not produced. It is not born as something produced, but by *genesis spontanea,* it is originary generation."[11] This pure spontaneity is an impression. It creates nothing. The new now is not a being, is not an object produced, and every language fails to describe this pure movement except by means of metaphor, that is, by borrowing its concepts from <94> the order of objects of experience that this temporalization makes possible. Husserl constantly warns us against these metaphors.* The process by means of which the living now, producing itself <95> by spontaneous generation,

---

* See, for example, the admirable §36 of *The Phenomenology of Internal Time-Consciousness,* which demonstrates the absence of a proper name for this strange "movement," which moreover is not a movement. "For all of that," Husserl concludes, "names fail us." We would still have to radicalize Husserl's intention here in a specific direction. For it is no accident if he still designates this unnameable as "absolute subjectivity," that is, as a being thought by starting from presence as substance, *ousia, hypokeimenon:* a self-identical being in self-presence, the self-presence making a subject out of the substance. What is said to be unnameable in this section is not literally something about which we know that it is a being that is *present* in the form of self-presence, a substance modified into a subject, into the absolute subject, whose self-presence is pure and depends on no external affection, on no outside. *All of that is present and we can name it; its proof is that we cannot put into question the being possessed by absolute subjectivity.* What are unnameable, according to Husserl, are only the "absolute properties" of this subject, which is therefore indeed designated according to the classical metaphysical schema that distinguishes the substance (the present being) from its attributes. Another schema that keeps the incomparable depth of analysis within the closure of the metaphysics of presence is the subject-object opposition. This being for whom the "absolute properties" are indescribable is present as *absolute* subjectivity, is a being that is *absolutely* present and *absolutely* present to itself, only in its opposition to the object. The object is relative; the subject is absolute: "We are unable to express this in any other way than: *we describe this flow in this way according to what is constituted,* but it consists in nothing that is temporally 'objective.' This is absolute subjectivity, and it has the absolute properties of something that we have to designate metaphorically as 'flow,' something that springs up 'now,' in a point of actuality, an originary source-point, etc. In the lived-experience of actuality, we have the originary source-point and a continuity of moments of retentions. For all of that, names fail us" (*The Phenomenology of Internal Time-Consciousness,* §36, my emphasis). <Translator: The equivalent passage can be found on page 100 of the Churchill translation.> Therefore the determination of "absolute subjectivity" would also have to be erased as soon as we think the present on the basis of différance and not the reverse. The concept of *subjectivity* belongs *a priori and in general* to the order of the *constituted.* This holds *a fortiori* for the analogical appresentation that constitutes intersubjectivity. Intersubjectivity is inseparable from temporalization as the openness of the present to an outside-of-itself, to an *other* absolute present. This outside-of-itself of time is its *spacing:* an *archi-scene.* This scene, as the relation of a present to an other present *as such,* that is, as non-derived re-presentation (*Vergegenwärtigung* or *Repräsentation*), produces the structure of the sign in general as "referral," as being-for-something (*für etwas sein*) and radically forbids its reduction. There is no constituting subjectivity. And it is necessary to deconstruct all the way down to the concept of constitution.

must, in order to be a now, be retained in another now, must affect itself, without empirical recourse, with a new originary actuality in which it will become a non-now as a past now, etc.; and such a process is indeed a pure auto-affection in which the same is the same only by affecting itself with an other, by becoming the other of the same. This auto-affection must be pure since the originary impression is affected there by nothing other than by itself, by the absolute "novelty" of another originary impression which is another now. As soon as we insert a determinate being into the description of this "movement," we are speaking by metaphor. We say the "movement" with the terms for what the "movement" makes possible. But we have always already drifted into ontic metaphor. Temporalization is the root of a metaphor that can be only originary. The word "time" itself, such as it has always been understood in the history of metaphysics, is a metaphor that indicates and dissimulates *at the same time* the "movement" of this auto-affection. All the concepts of metaphysics—in particular those of activity and passivity, will and non-will, and therefore those of affection or auto-affection, of purity and impurity, etc.—*cover over and coincide* with the strange "movement" of this difference.

But this pure difference, which constitutes the self-presence of the living present, reintroduces into it originarily all the impurity that we had believed we were able to exclude from it. The living present arises on the basis of its non-self-identity, and on the basis of the retentional trace. It is always already a trace. This trace is unthinkable if we start from the simplicity of a present whose life would be interior to itself. The self of the living present is originarily a trace. The trace is not an attribute about which we could say that the self of the living present "is originarily" the trace. It is necessary to think originary-being from the trace and not the trace from originary-being. This archi-writing is at work in the origin of sense. Since sense, as Husserl has recognized, has a temporal nature, it is never simply <96> present. It is always already engaged in the "movement" of the trace, that is, in the order of "signification." Sense has always already exited from itself into the "expressive stratum" of lived-experience. Since the trace is the relation of intimacy of the living present to its outside, the openness to exteriority in general, to the non-proper, etc., *the temporalization of sense is from the very beginning "spacing."* As soon as we admit spacing at once as "interval" or difference and as openness to the outside, there is no absolute interiority. The "outside" insinuates itself into the movement by means of which the inside of non-space, which bears the name "time," appears to itself, constitutes itself, and "presents" itself. Space is "in" time. It is the pure exiting of time to the outside of itself. It is outside-of-itself as the self-relation of time. The exteriority of space, exteriority as space, does not take time by surprise. Exteriority opens itself as the pure "outside" "in" the movement of temporalization. If we now remember that the pure interiority of phonic auto-affection assumed the purely temporal nature of the "expressive" process, we see that the theme of a pure interiority of speech or of "hearing-oneself-speak" is radically contradicted by "time" itself. Even the exiting "into the world" is also originarily implied by the movement of temporalization. "Time" cannot be an "absolute subjectivity" precisely because we are not able to think it on the basis of the present and on the basis of the presence to itself of a present being. Like everything that is thought under this heading and like everything that is excluded by the most rigorous transcendental reduction, the "world" is originarily implied by the movement of temporalization. Like the relation between an inside and an outside in general, an existent and a non-existent in general, a constituter and a constituted in general, temporalization is at once the very power and the very limit of the phenomenological reduction. Hearing-oneself-speak is not the interiority of an inside closed in upon itself. It is the irreducible openness in the inside, the eye and the world in speech. The phenomenological reduction is a scene.

<97> Also, just as expression does not come to be added on as a "stratum"* to the presence of a pre-expressive sense, the outside of indication does not come to affect accidentally the inside of expression. Their interweaving (*Verflechtung*) is originary. The intertwining is not the kind of contingent association that methodical care and a patient reduction could undo. Even as necessary as the analysis is, it encounters here an absolute limit. If indication is not added onto expression which is not added onto sense, we can nevertheless speak, in regard to them, about an originary "supplement." Their addition comes to supplement a lack, an originary non-self-presence. And if indication, for example, writing in the everyday sense, must necessarily "add itself" onto speech in order to complete the constitution of the ideal object, if speech must "add itself" onto the identity of the object in thought, this is because the "presence" of sense and of speech has already begun to be lacking in regard to itself.

---

* In the important §124 to §127 of *Ideas I,* which we shall follow elsewhere step by step, Husserl invites us, while continuously speaking of a substratum of pre-expressive lived-experience, not "to expect too much from this image of stratification [Sc*hichtung*]." Husserl says, "Expression is not a sort of overlaid varnish or covering garment; it is a spiritual formation that exercises new intentional functions on the intentional substratum [*Unterschicht*]." <Translator: The equivalent passage from §124 can be found on page 297 of the Kersten translation of *Ideas I.* When Derrida says that he will follow these sections step by step elsewhere, he is referring to "Form and Meaning," collected in *Margins of Philosophy.*>

7

The Originative Supplement

<98> Thus understood, supplementarity is really *différance*, the operation of differing that, at once, splits and delays presence, subjecting it by the same action to originary division and originary delay. Différance is to be thought prior to the separation between deferral <*différer*> as delay and differing <*différer*> as the active work of difference <*différence*>. It must be understood that différance is unthinkable starting from consciousness, that is, starting from presence, or starting simply from the opposite of presence, absence or non-consciousness. It is also unthinkable as the simple *homogeneous* complication of a diagram or a line of time, as complex "succession." Supplementary différance vicariates for presence in its originary lack in regard to itself. We must now verify, *going through* the First Logical Investigation, in what way these concepts respect the relation between the sign in general (indicative as much as expressive) and presence in general. *Going through* Husserl's text, that is, in a reading that can be simply neither that of commentary nor that of interpretation.

Let us first note that this concept of originary supplementarity not only implies the non-fullness of presence (or in Husserl's language, the non-fulfillment of an intuition), it also designates this function of substitutive supplementing in general, the structure of the "in the place of" (*für etwas*) that belongs to every sign in general and about which at the beginning we were astonished that Husserl subjected <99> the possibility of this structure to no critical question, taking its possibility for granted when he distinguished between the indicative sign and the expressive sign. What we would like finally to start thinking about is the fact that the for-itself of self-presence (*für-sich*), traditionally determined in its dative dimension as phenomenological, reflective, or pre-reflective auto-donation, arises in the movement of supplementarity as originary substitution, in the form of the "in the place of" (*für etwas*), that is, as we have seen, in the very operation of signification in general. The *for-itself* would be an *in-the-place-of-itself*: put *for itself*, in the place of itself. The strange structure of the supplement appears here: a possibility produces by delay that to which it is said to be added.

This structure of supplementarity is very complicated. Insofar as it is a supplement, the signifier does not first re-present merely the absent signified. It substitutes itself for another signifier, for another signifying order, which carries on another relation with the missing presence, another relation that is more valuable owing to the play of difference. It is more valuable since the play of difference is the movement of idealization and because the more the signifier is ideal, the more it augments the potency of repetition of presence, the more it protects, reserves, and capitalizes on sense. In this way, the indication is not only the substitute that supplements the absence or the invisibility of the indicated. The indicated, as we remember, is always an *existent*. The indication also replaces another type of signifier: the expressive sign, that is, a signifier whose signified (the *Bedeutung*) is ideal. In fact, in real, communicative, etc. discourse, expression yields its place to indication because, as we recall, the sense intended by another and, in a general way, the lived-experience of another are not and can never be present in person. This is why, as Husserl says, expression then functions "as indication."

We still need to know now—and this is most important—in what way expression itself implies in its structure a non-fullness. Expression is known, however, as being fuller than indication <100> since the appresentational detour is no longer necessary to it, and because it could function as such in the alleged self-presence of solitary discourse.

In fact, it is indeed important to measure at what distance—at what articulated distance—an intuitionistic theory of knowledge governs Husserl's concept of language. The entire originality of this concept depends on the fact that its final subjection to intuitionism does not oppress what we could call the freedom of language, the outspokenness of a discourse, even if it is false and contradictory. One is able to speak without knowing. Against the entire philosophical tradition, Husserl demonstrates that speech then is still fully legitimate speech provided that it is obedient to certain rules which are not immediately given as rules of knowledge. Pure logical grammar, the pure morphology of significations, must tell us *a priori* under what conditions a discourse can be a discourse, even if it makes no knowledge possible.

We must here consider the final exclusion—or reduction—to which Husserl brings us in order to isolate the specific purity of expression. This is his most audacious exclusion. It consists in putting out of play, as "unessential components" of expression, the acts of intuitive knowledge that "fulfill" the meaning <*vouloir-dire*>.

We know that the act of meaning, the one that gives the *Bedeutung* (*Bedeutungsintention*), is always the aim of a relation to the object. But it is enough that this intention animates the body of a signifier for that discourse to take place. The fulfillment of the intention by an intuition is not indispensable. It belongs to the original structure of expression to be able to do without the full presence of the object aimed at in intuition.

Evoking once more the confusion which is born from the entanglement (*Verflechtung*) of relations, Husserl writes (in §9):

> If we seek to plant ourselves firmly in the soil of pure description, the concrete phenomenon of expression animated with a sense [*sinnebelebten*] is articulated, on the one hand, into a *physical phenomenon* in which the expression <101> is constituted according to its physical side, and on the other hand, into *acts* which endow it with the *Bedeutung* and contingently *intuitive fullness,* in which the relation to the expressed objective correlate is constituted. Thanks to these acts, expression is more than a simple *flatus vocis.* It *intends* something, and insofar as expression intends something, it is related to something objective.[1]

Fullness is therefore merely contingent. The absence of the intended object does not compromise the meaning; the absence does not reduce the expression to its unanimated and in itself meaningless physical side. Husserl writes,

> This objective something [to which the intention relates itself] can or indeed does appear as actually present [*aktuell gegenwärtig*] thanks to the accompanying or at least represented [*vergegenwärtig*] intuitions (for example in an imaginary form). In the case where that has taken place, the relation to the objective correlate is realized. Or else, when this is not the case, the expression functions with its charge of sense [*fungiert sinnvoll*], and is always more than a simple *flatus vocis,* although it is deprived of the intuition that founds it, which provides it with an object.[2]

The "fulfilling" intuition is not therefore essential to the expression, to the intention of the meaning. The rest of this chapter is devoted to accumulating proofs of this difference between intention and intuition. Since all classical theories of language have been blind to the difference,[*][3] they have been unable to avoid aporias and absurdities. These, Husserl marks out as he proceeds. Over the course of subtle and decisive analyses that we are unable to follow here, the demonstration is given of the ideality of the *Bedeutung* and of the non-coincidence between the *expression,* the *Bedeutung* (both insofar as they are ideal unities), and the *object.* Two iden-

---

* According to Husserl, of course. This is undoubtedly truer of the modern theories that he refutes than, for example, certain medieval attempts to which he hardly ever refers. The exception is a brief allusion, in *Formal and Transcendental Logic,* to Thomas of Erfurt's *Grammatica speculativa.*

tical expressions can have the same *Bedeutung,* meaning the same thing and yet having a different object (for example, in the two propositions "Bucephalus is a *horse*" and "This steed is a *horse*"). Two different expressions <102> are able to have different *Bedeutungen,* but intend the same object (for example, in the two expressions "The victor at Jena" and "The vanquished at Waterloo"). Finally, two different expressions are able to have the same *Bedeutung* and the same object (*Londres,* London, *zwei,* two, *duo,* etc.).

Without such distinctions, no pure logical grammar would be possible. Consequently, the pure morphology of judgments, whose possibility supports the entire structure of *Formal and Transcendental Logic,* would be forbidden. In fact, we know that pure logical grammar depends entirely on the distinction between *Widersinnigkeit* and *Sinnlosigkeit.* If it is obedient to certain rules, an expression can be *widersinnig* (contradictory, false, absurd according to a certain type of absurdity) while still having an intelligible sense that allows a normal discourse to take place, without becoming non-sense (*Unsinn*). It can have no possible object for empirical reasons (a golden mountain) or for *a priori* reasons (a square circle) while still having an intelligible sense, without being *sinnlos.* The absence of the object (*Gegenstandlosigkeit*) is not therefore the absence of meaning (*Bedeutungslosigkeit*). Pure logical grammar therefore excludes from the normalcy of discourse only non-sense in the sense of *Unsinn* (*Abracadabra, vert est ou*).[4] If we were not able to understand what "square circle" or "golden mountain" *means,* how could we come to a conclusion about the absence of a possible object? In *Unsinn,* in the a-grammaticality of non-sense, this minimum of understanding is denied to us.

Following the logic and necessity of these distinctions, we might be tempted to support the idea not only that the meaning does not essentially imply the intuition of the object, but also that it essentially excludes the intuition. The structural originality of the meaning would be the *Gegenstandlosigkeit,* the absence of the object given to intuition. In the fullness of the presence that comes to fulfill the aim of the meaning, intuition and intention fuse into one another; they "form a unity of intimate <103> merging [*eine innig verschmolzene Einheit*] that has an original character."[*] This is to say that the language that speaks in the presence

---

[*] "In the realized relation of the expression to its objective correlate, the expression that is animated with sense becomes one [*eint sich*] with the acts of the fulfillment of the *Bedeutung.* The phonic sonority of the word is first made one with [*ist eins mit*] the intention of *Bedeutung,* and this in its turn is made one (as intentions in general are made one with their fulfillments) with the corresponding fulfillment of *Bedeutung*" (§9). <Translator: The equivalent passage can be found on page 192 of the English translation, volume 1. The French quote has "ist einst mit," but this phrase appears to be a typographical error.> At

of its object erases or lets its own originality dissolve; it erases this structure that belongs only to it and that allows it to function *all alone* when its intention is severed from intuition. Here, instead of suspecting that Husserl begins the analysis with its dissociation too soon, we might wonder if he is not unifying too much and too soon. Is it not excluded, for essential and structural reasons—the very reasons that Husserl recalls— that the unity of intuition and intention are ever homogeneous and that the meaning fuses into intuition without disappearing? Is it not the case that we will never in principle be able, *in expression,* "to honor the draft drawn on intuition," here taking up Husserl's language?[5]

Let us consider the extreme case of a "statement about perception." Let us suppose that it is produced in the very moment of perceptual intuition. I say, "I see now a particular person by the window," at the moment I actually see that person. What is implied structurally in what I am doing is that the content of this expression is ideal and that its unity is not impaired by the absence of the *hic et nunc* perception.[*,6] The one who, next to me or at an infinite distance in time and space, hears this proposition must, in principle, understand what I intend to say. Since this possibility is the possibility of discourse, it must structure the very act of the one who speaks <104> while perceiving. My non-perception, my non-intuition, my *hic et nunc* absence are said by that which I say, by *what* I say and *because* I say it. Never will this structure be able to make with intuition a "unity of intimate merging." The absence of intuition—and therefore of the subject of the intuition—is not only *tolerated* by the discourse, the absence is *required* by the structure of signification in general, were one to consider it *in itself.* The absence is radically required: the total absence of the subject and of the object of the statement—the death of the writer and/or the disappearance of the objects that he has been able to describe—does not prevent a text from "meaning" <*vouloir-dire*>. On the contrary, this possibility gives birth to meaning <*vouloir-dire*> as such, hands it over to being heard and being read.

Let us go further. In what way is writing—the common name for signs that function despite the total absence of the subject, by means of

---

the beginning of §10, Husserl will still specify that this unity is not a simple "being-together" in simultaneity but "a unity of intimate confusion." <Translator: The English translation says (page 193): "The above distinguished acts involving the expression's appearance, on the one hand, and the meaning-intention, on the other, do not constitute a mere aggregate of simultaneously given items in consciousness. They rather form an intimately fused unity of peculiar character.">

* "In the statement of a perception, we distinguish, as for every statement, between *content* and *object,* and we do this in such a way that by content we understand the self-identical *Bedeutung* that the hearer can grasp even if he himself is not perceiving" (§14).

(and beyond) his death—implied in the very movement of signification in general, in particular, in speech that is called "live"? In what way does writing inaugurate and complete idealization, being itself neither real nor ideal? Finally, in what way are death, idealization, repetition, and signification thinkable, in their pure possibility, only on the basis of one and the same openness? This time, let us take the example of the personal pronoun "I." Husserl classifies it among the expressions that are "essentially occasional." It shares this characteristic with a whole "group presenting a conceptual unity of possible *Bedeutungen,* such that it is essential for this expression to orient its actual *Bedeutung* each time to the occasion, to the person who is speaking, or his situation."[7] This group is distinguished at once from the group of expressions whose plurivocity is contingent and reducible by means of a convention (the word "rule," for example, means both a wooden instrument and a prescription), and from the group of "objective" expressions whose univocity the discursive circumstances, context, and situation of the speaking subject do not affect (for example, "all the expressions in theory, expressions out of which the principles and theorems, the proofs <105> and theories of the 'abstract' sciences are made up." The mathematical expression is the model for this group).[8] Only these objective expressions are absolutely pure of indicative contamination. We are able to recognize an essentially occasional expression by means of the fact that we cannot in principle replace it in the discourse by a permanent, objective, conceptual representation without distorting the *Bedeutung* of the statement. If, for example, I tried to substitute for the word "I," such as it appears in a statement, with what I believe to be its objective conceptual content ("whatever person who, while speaking, is designating himself"), I would end up in absurdities. Instead of "I am pleased," I would have "whatever person who, while speaking, is designating himself is pleased." Each time that such a substitution distorts the statement, we are dealing with an essentially subjective and occasional expression, whose function remains indicative. Thus indication penetrates wherever a reference in the discourse to the situation of the subject does not let itself be reduced, wherever the situation of the subject lets itself be indicated by a personal pronoun, a demonstrative pronoun, or a "subjective" adverb of the following type: "here," "there," "above," "below," "now," "yesterday," "tomorrow," "before," "after," etc. This massive return of indication into expression forces Husserl to conclude:

> An essentially indicating character naturally spreads to all expressions which include these and similar representations as parts: this includes all the multiple forms of discourse where the speaker gives normal

expression to something concerning himself, or which is thought of in relation to himself. All expressions for perceptions, convictions, doubts, wishes, fears, commands belong here.[9]

The root of all of these expressions, as we see very quickly, is the zero-point of the subjective origin, the "I," the "here," the "now." The *Bedeutung* of these expressions is carried off into indication each time that it animates a real discourse for others. But Husserl seems to think that for *the one who speaks* this *Bedeutung*, as the relation to <106> the object (I, here, now), is "realized."* Husserl says, "In solitary discourse, the *Bedeutung* of the 'I' is realized essentially in the immediate representation of our own personality. . . ."

Is this certain? Even if we assume that such an immediate representation is possible and actually given, does not the appearance of the word "I" in solitary discourse (a supplement whose reason for being is moreover not clear if the immediate representation is possible) already function as an ideality? Consequently, does not the appearance of the word "I" offer itself as able to remain *the same* for an I-here-now in general, keeping its sense even if my empirical presence is erased or is modified radically? When I say "I," even in solitary discourse, am I able to endow my statement with sense in any other way than by implying in it, as always, the possible absence of the object of the discourse, in this case, myself? When I say "I am" to myself, this expression, as with every expression according to Husserl, has the status of being discourse only if it is intelligible in the absence of the object, in the absence of the intuitive presence, therefore in this case, in the absence of myself. Moreover, it is in this way that the *ergo sum* is introduced into the philosophical tradition and a discourse on the transcendental ego is possible. Whether or not I have the actual intuition of myself, "I" does express. Whether or not I am living, the words "I am" "mean" *<veulent dire>*. Here too the fulfilling intuition is not an "essential component" of the expression. Whether or not "I" functions in solitary discourse, with or without the self-presence of the speaking being, it is *sinnvoll*. And one has <107> no need of know-

---

* "In solitary discourse, the *Bedeutung* of the "I" is realized essentially in the immediate representation of our own personality, which is also the meaning of the word in communicative discourse. Each interlocutor has his I-representation (and with his individual concept of the "I") and this is why the word's *Bedeutung* differs with each individual." One cannot help being astonished in the face of this *individual concept* and this *Bedeutung* which differ with each individual. And Husserl's premises themselves encourage the astonishment. Husserl pursues the idea by saying, "But since each person, by speaking of himself, says 'I,' the word has the character of a universally operative indexical of this fact."

ing who is speaking in order to understand it or even to utter it. Once more, the border appears hardly certain between solitary discourse and communication, between the reality and the representation of the discourse. Does Husserl not contradict what he established in regard to the difference between *Gegenstandlosigkeit*[10] and *Bedeutungslosigkeit* when he writes: "The word 'I' names a different person from case to case, and does so by way of an always new *Bedeutung*"? Do not discourse and the ideal nature of every *Bedeutung* exclude that a *Bedeutung* is "always new"? Does Husserl not contradict what he asserted about the independence of the intention and the fulfilling intuition by writing: "What constitutes each time its *Bedeutung* (that of the word 'I') can be drawn only from the living discourse and intuitive givens that participate in it. When we read this word without knowing who has written it, we have a word, if not deprived of *Bedeutung*, at least foreign to its normal *Bedeutung*."[11] *Husserl's premises should authorize us to say exactly the opposite.* Just as I do not need to perceive in order to understand a perceptual statement, I do not need the intuition of the object "I" in order to understand the word "I." The possibility of this non-intuition constitutes the *Bedeutung* as such, the *normal Bedeutung* as such. When the word "I" appears, the ideality of its *Bedeutung*, insofar as it is distinct from its "object," puts us in the situation that Husserl describes as abnormal: as if the word "I" were written by someone unknown. Only this situation allows us to account for the fact that we understand the word "I" not only when its "author" is unknown, but also when he is perfectly fictional—and when he is dead. The ideality of the *Bedeutung* has here a value that is structurally testimonial. And just as the value of a perceptual statement depended on neither the actuality nor the possibility of the perception, the signifying value of the "I" does not depend on the life of the speaking subject. Whether the perception accompanies or not the perceptual statement, whether life as self-presence accompanies or not the statement <108> of the "I," this is perfectly indifferent to the functioning of the meaning. My death is structurally necessary to pronouncing the "I." Whether I am also "living" and whether I am certain about being alive, that comes over and above the movement of the meaning. And this structure is active. It keeps its original efficacy even when I say "I am living" at the precise moment when, if that is possible, I have its full and actual intuition. The *Bedeutung* "I am" or "I am living," or even "my living present is," is what it is, it has the ideal identity proper to all *Bedeutung* only if it does not let itself be impaired by falsehood, that is, if I can be dead at the moment during which it functions. Undoubtedly, it will be different from the *Bedeutung* "I am dead," but not necessarily from the *fact* that "I am dead." The statement "I am living" is accompanied by my being-dead and the statement's possibility requires the possibility that I be dead—and the reverse. This is not an extraordinary story by Poe, but the ordinary story of language.[12] Earlier, we gained access to the "I am mortal" from the "I am." Here we understand the "I am" from the "I am dead." The anonymity of the written "I," the impropriety of the "I write" is, contrary to what Husserl says, the normal situation. The autonomy of the meaning in regard to intuitive knowledge, the autonomy that Husserl demonstrates and that we were calling earlier the freedom of language, "outspokenness," has its norm in writing and the relation to death. This writing is not able to come as added onto speech because as soon as speech awakens writing has doubled it by animating it. Here indication neither degrades nor diverts expression; indication dictates it. We are drawing this conclusion from the idea of pure logical grammar, from the rigorous distinction between the intention of the meaning (*Bedetungsintention*) which can always function "emptily" and its "contingent" fulfillment by the intuition of the object. This conclusion is reinforced even more by the supplementary distinction, which is also rigorous, between the fulfillment by the "sense" and the fulfillment by the "object." The former does not necessarily demand the latter, and we could draw the same lesson from a careful reading of §14 ("Content <109> as Object, Content as Fulfilling Sense and Content as Simple Sense or *Bedeutung*").

Why does Husserl refuse to draw these conclusions from the same premises? The motive for full "presence," the intuitionist imperative and the project of knowledge continue to govern—at a distance, let us say— the whole of the description. In one and the same movement, Husserl describes and erases the emancipation of discourse as non-knowledge. The originality of the meaning as an aim is limited by the *telos* of vision. The difference that separates intention from intuition, in order to be radical, would nevertheless be *pro-visional*. And, despite everything, this pro-vision would constitute the essence of meaning <*vouloir-dire*>. The *eidos* is determined in depth by the *telos*. The "symbol" always signals toward the "truth" whose lack it is constituted as:

> If the "possibility" or the "truth" happens to be lacking, the intention of
> the statement is obviously achieved only "symbolically"; it cannot derive
> the fullness which constitutes its epistemological value from intuition
> or from the categorial functions which must be exercised in its founda-
> tion. It then lacks, as one says, a "true," an "authentic" *Bedeutung*.[13]

In other words, the true and authentic meaning is the wanting to say-the-truth.[14] This subtle shift is the resumption of the *eidos* in the *telos* and of language in knowledge. A discourse may have already conformed to its discursive essence when it was false, but it nevertheless attains its entelechy when it is true. One can well *speak* by saying "the circle is square," but one speaks *well* by saying that the circle is not square. There is already sense in the first proposition. But we would be wrong to infer from it that the sense *does not await* the truth. It does not wait for the truth insofar as it expects it; it precedes the truth only as its anticipation. *In truth,* the *telos* that announces the achievement that is promised for "later" has already, earlier, opened up the sense as the relation to the object. This is what the concept of *normalcy* means each time that it intervenes in Husserl's descriptions. The <110> norm is knowledge, the intuition that is adequate to its object, the evidence that is not only distinct but "clear": the full presence of the sense to a consciousness that is itself present to itself in the fullness of its life, in the fullness of its living present. Also, without overlooking the rigor and the audacity of the "pure logical grammar," without forgetting the advantages that it can offer if we compare it to the classical projects of rational grammar, it is indeed necessary to acknowledge that its "formality" is limited. We could say as much about the pure morphology of *judgments,* which, in *Formal and Transcendental Logic,* determines the pure logical grammar or pure morphology of *significations.* The purification of the formal is regulated according to a concept of *sense* that is itself determined on the basis of a *relation to the object.* The form is always the form of a sense, and the sense is open only in the epistemological intentionality of the relation to an object. The form is only the empty, pure intention of this intentionality. Perhaps no project of pure grammar escapes it, perhaps the *telos* of epistemological rationality is the irreducible origin of the idea of pure grammar, perhaps the semantic theme, as "empty" as it is, always limits the formalist project. Always in Husserl, the transcendental intuitionism weighs very heavily on the formalist theme. Apparently independent of the fulfilling intuitions, the "pure" forms of signification are always, insofar as they are "empty" or crossed out, regulated by the epistemological criterion of a relation to the object. The difference between "the circle is square" and "green is or" or "abracadabra" (and Husserl a bit quickly associates these last two examples and is perhaps not careful enough in regard to their difference) consists in the fact that the form of a relation to the object and of a unitary intuition appears only in the first example. This aim will always be disappointed here, but this proposition makes *sense* only because *another content,* being whispered in this form (S is P), *could* provide us with an object to be known and seen. The "circle is square," an expression endowed with sense (*sinnvoll*), has no possible object, but it makes <111> sense only to the extent that its grammatical form tolerates the possibility of a relation to the object. The efficacy and the form of signs that do not obey these rules, that is, that promise no knowledge, can be determined as non-sense (*Unsinn*) only if we have already, according to the most traditional philosophical gesture, defined sense in general on the basis of truth as objectivity. Otherwise, we would have to throw away into absolute nonsense all poetical language that transgresses and does not let itself ever be reduced to the laws of this grammar of knowledge. Within the forms of non-discursive signification (music and non-literary arts in general) as well as in discourses of the type "abracadabra" or "green is or," there are resources of sense which do not signal toward the possible object. Husserl would not deny the signifying force of such formations; he would simply not grant them the formal quality of expressions endowed with *sense,* that is, the formal quality of logic as the relation to an *object.* Recognizing this is to recognize the initial limitation of sense to knowledge, of the *logos* to objectivity, of language to reason.

* * *

We have put to the test the systematic solidarity of the concepts of sense, ideality, objectivity, truth, intuition, perception, and expression. Their common matrix is being as *presence:* the absolute proximity of self-identity; the being-in-front of the object in its availability for repetition; the maintaining of the temporal present, the ideal form of which is the self-presence of transcendental *life* whose ideal identity allows *idealiter* repetition to infinity. The living-present, which is a concept that cannot be decomposed into a subject and an attribute, is therefore the founding concept of phenomenology as metaphysics.

However, since all of what is *purely* thought under this concept is by the same token determined as *ideality,* the living-present is *in fact* really, factually, etc. deferred to infinity. This différance is <112> the difference between ideality and non-ideality. This is a proposition that we could have ascertained already at the beginning of the *Logical Investigations,* from the point of view that concerns us. Thus, after having proposed an essential distinction between objective expressions and expressions that are essentially subjective, Husserl shows that absolute ideality can be only on the side of objective expressions. There is nothing surprising in that. But he adds immediately that even in essentially subjective expressions, the fluctuation is not in the objective content of the expression (the *Bedeutung*), but only in the act of meaning (*bedeuten* <*vouloir-dire:* wanting-to-say>). This allows him to conclude, apparently against his earlier demonstration, that in a subjective expression, the *content* can always be replaced by an objective content which is therefore ideal. Only the act is then lost to ideality. But this substitution (which, let us note in passing, would still confirm what we were saying about the play of life and death in the "I") is ideal. Since the ideal is always thought by Husserl in the form of the Idea in the Kantian sense, this substitution of ideality for non-ideality, of objectivity for non-objectivity, is *deferred to infinity*. Attributing a subjective origin to the fluctuation, contesting the theory according to which the fluctuation would belong to the objective content of the *Bedeutung*, and would thus undermine its ideality, Husserl writes,

> We shall have to look on such a conception as invalid. The content that the subjective expression orienting its *Bedeutung* according to the situation aims at is an ideal unit of *Bedeutung* in precisely the same sense as the content of a fixed expression. This is shown by the fact that, ideally speaking, each subjective expression is replaceable by an objective expression which will preserve the identity of each momentary *Bedeutung*. *Truly, we shall have to recognize that this substitution cannot be effectuated not only for reasons of practical necessity, for example, because of its complexity, but also that, to a large degree, it is not realizable in fact and even that it will remain* <113> *always unrealizable.* Clearly, in fact, to say that each subjective expression could be replaced by an objective expression is no more than to assert the *absence of limits [Schrankenlosigkeit] of objective reason.* Everything that is, can be known "in itself." Its being is a being definite in content, and documented in such and such "truths in themselves." . . . But what is objectively quite definite, must permit *objective* determination, and what permits objective determination, must, ideally speaking, permit expression through wholly determinate word *Bedeutungen.* . . . *But we are infinitely distant from this ideal.* . . . *Strike out the essentially occasional expressions from one's language, try to describe any subjective experience in a univocal and objectively stable way: such an attempt of this kind is obviously vain.*[15]

"The Origin of Geometry" will take up in a form that is literally identical these propositions concerning the univocity of the objective expression as an inaccessible ideal.

In its ideal value, the whole system of the "essential distinctions" is therefore a purely teleological structure. By the same token, the possibility of distinguishing between sign and non-sign, between the linguistic sign and the non-linguistic sign, expression and indication, ideality and non-ideality, between subject and object, grammaticality and non-grammaticality, pure grammaticality and empirical grammaticality, pure general grammaticality and pure logical grammaticality, intention and intuition, etc.: this pure possibility is deferred to infinity. Thereupon, these "essential distinctions" are gripped by the following aporia: *in fact, realiter,* they are never respected, and Husserl recognizes this. *In principle and idealiter,* they are erased since they only live as distinctions from the difference between principle and fact, ideality and reality. Their possibility is their impossibility.

<114> But how does this difference give itself to be thought? What does "to infinity" mean here? What does presence as différance to infinity mean? What does the life of the living present as différance to infinity mean?

That Husserl has always thought infinity as an Idea in the Kantian sense, as the indefiniteness of a "to infinity," that makes us believe that he has never *derived* difference from the fullness of a *parousia,* from the full presence of a positive infinite, that he has never believed in the achievement of an "absolute knowledge" as presence nearby to itself, in the *Logos,* in the achievement of an infinite concept. And what he shows us in regard to the movement of temporalization leaves no doubt on this matter: although he has not made "articulation" his theme, namely, the "diacritical" work of difference in the constitution of sense and of the sign, in depth he recognizes the necessity of doing this. And yet the entire phenomenological discourse is, as we have seen, gripped by the schema of a metaphysics of presence which relentlessly exhausts itself trying to make difference derivative. Within this schema, Hegelianism seems more radical: *par excellence* at the point where it brings to light that the positive infinite must be thought (which is possible only if it thinks *itself*) so that the indefiniteness of différance may appear *as such.* Hegel's criticism of Kant would no doubt also be valid against Husserl. But this appearing of the Ideal as infinite différance can only be produced in a relationship to death in general. Only a relationship to my-death can make the infinite différance of presence appear. By the same token, compared to the ideality of the positive infinite, this relation to my-death becomes an accident of finite empiricity. The appearing of infinite différance is itself finite. Différance, which is nothing outside of this relationship, thereupon becomes the finitude of life as the essential relation to itself as to its death. *The infinite différance is finite.* We are no longer able to think it within the opposition of the finite and the infinite, absence and presence, negation and affirmation.

<115> In this sense, *within* the metaphysics of presence, of philosophy as the knowledge of the presence of the object, as knowing's being-nearby-itself in consciousness, we believe quite simply in absolute knowledge as the *closure* if not the end of history. We believe in it literally—*and that such a closure has taken place.* The history of being as presence, as self-presence in absolute knowledge, as consciousness (of) self in the infinity of *parousia,* this history is closed. The history of presence

is closed, for "history" has never meant anything but this: presentation (*Gegenwärtigung*) of being <*l'être*>, production and gathering of the being <*l'étant*> in presence, as knowledge and mastery. Since full presence has the *vocation* of infinity as absolute presence to itself in con-sciousness, the achievement of absolute knowledge is the end of the infinite which can only be the unity of the concept, *logos*, and consciousness in a voice without différance. *The history of metaphysics is the absolute wanting-to-hear-itself speak.* This history is closed when this absolute infinity appears to itself as its own death. *A voice without différance, a voice without writing is at once absolutely alive and absolutely dead.*

As for what "begins" then "beyond" absolute knowledge, *unheard-of* thoughts are required, thoughts that are sought across the memory of old signs. As long as différance remains a concept about which we ask ourselves whether it must be thought from presence or prior to it, it remains one of these old signs. And it tells us that it is necessary to continue indefinitely to interrogate presence within the closure of knowledge. It is necessary to hear it in this way and otherwise—otherwise, that is, within the openness of an unheard-of question that opens itself neither onto knowledge nor onto a non-knowledge as knowledge to come. In the openness of this question, *we no longer know.* This does not mean that we know nothing, but that we are beyond absolute knowledge (and its ethical, aesthetic, or religious system), approaching that on the basis of which its closure is announced and decided. Such a question will be legitimately heard <116> as *wanting to say nothing*, as no longer belonging to the system of wanting-to-say.

We no longer know therefore whether what is always presented as the derived and modified re-presentation of simple presentation, as the "supplement," as "sign," "writing," "trace," "is" not, in a sense necessarily but in a new way a-historical, "older" than presence and the system of truth, older than "history"—"older" than sense and the senses, older than the originary donating intuition, than the actual and full perception of the "thing itself," older than vision, hearing, touch, even before one distinguishes between their "sensible" literality and their metaphorical appearance in the scene of the entire history of philosophy. We no longer know therefore whether what has always been reduced and abased as an accident, modification, and re-turn in the old names of "sign" and of "re-presentation" has not repressed what would relate truth to its own death as to its origin, whether the force of *Vergegenwärtigung* in which the *Gegenwärtigung*[16] is de-presented in order to be re-presented as such, whether the force of repetition of the living present which re-presents itself in a *supplement* because it has never been present to itself, whether what we call the old names of force and différance, is not more "ancient" than the "originary."

In order to think this age, in order to "speak" of it, other names would be necessary than those of sign or re-presentation. And it is necessary to think as "normal" and pre-originary what Husserl believes he is able to isolate as a particular, accidental, dependent, and secondary experience: the experience of the indefinite drift of signs as errancy and change of scenes (*Verwandlung*), linking the re-presentations (*Vergegenwärtigungen*) to one another, without beginning or end. There has never been perception, and "presentation" is a representation of representation that desires itself within representation as its birth or its death.

Everything no doubt began in this way: "A name uttered in front of us makes us think of the Dresden gallery. . . . We wander <117> through the rooms. . . . A picture by Teniers . . . represents a picture gallery. . . . The pictures in this gallery represent again pictures which for their part would make visible inscriptions that we are able to decipher, etc."[17]

Nothing has of course preceded this situation. Nothing will suspend it with security. It is not *comprehended*, as Husserl would like, among intuitions and presentations. Outside of the gallery, no perception of the full light of presence is given to us nor promised with security.[18] The gallery is the labyrinth, which includes its own ways out within itself. We have never fallen into it as into a particular *case*[19] of experience, the case that Husserl then believes he is describing.

Thus one still has to *speak*, to make the voice *resonate* in the corridors in order to supplement the shining forth of presence. The phoneme, the *akoumenon* is the *phenomenon of the labyrinth*. This is the *case* of the *phonē*. Soaring up to the sun of presence, it is the path of Icarus.

And contrary to what phenomenology—which is always a phenomenology of perception—has tried to make us believe, contrary to what our desire cannot not be tempted to believe, the thing itself always steals away.

Contrary to the assurance that Husserl gives us about it a little later, "the look" cannot "remain."[20]

Notes

Translator's Introduction

1. The first English translation of *La voix et le phénomène* was done by David B. Allison as *Speech and Phenomena* (Evanston, Ill.: Northwestern University Press, 1972); and for decades Derrida's book was known in the Anglophone world by the title *Speech and Phenomena.*

2. Jacques Derrida, *De la grammatologie* (Paris: Minuit, 1967); English translation by Gayatri Spivak as *Of Grammatology* (Baltimore: Johns Hopkins University Press, 1997, corrected edition).

3. Jacques Derrida, *L'écriture et la différance* (Paris: Seuil Points, 1967); English translation by Alan Bass as *Writing and Difference* (Chicago: University of Chicago Press, 1967).

4. See Jacques Derrida, "Ponctuations: Le temps de la these," in *Du droit à la philosophie* (Paris: Galilée, 1990), 452; English translation by Kathleen McLaughlin as "Punctuations: The Time of a Thesis," in *Eyes of the University: Right to Philosophy 2* (Stanford, Calif.: Stanford University Press, 2004), 123. The "Ponctuations" text dates from 1980.

5. Derrida's other books on Husserl are Edmund Husserl, *L'origine de la géométrie, traduction et introduction par Jacques Derrida* (Paris: Presses Universitaires de France, 1962); English translation by John P. Leavey, Jr., as *Edmund Husserl's "Origin of Geometry": An Introduction* (Lincoln: University of Nebraska Press, 1989 [1978]). Derrida then published his Mémoire (the equivalent of a master's thesis) from the academic year 1953–54 in 1990 as *Le problem de la genèse dans la philosophie de Husserl* (Paris: Presses Universitaires de France, 1990); English translation by Marian Hobson as *The Problem of Genesis in Husserl's Philosophy* (Chicago: University of Chicago Press, 2003). Derrida returned to Husserl again in 2000 in his *Le toucher—Jean-Luc Nancy* (Paris: Galilée, 2000), 183–208; English translation by Christine Irizarry as *On Touching—Jean-Luc Nancy* (Stanford, Calif.: Stanford University Press, 2005), 159–82.

6. See Michel Foucault, "La pensée du dehors," in *Dits et écrits I 1954–1975* (Paris: Quarto Gallimard, 2001), 546–67; English translation by Brian Massumi as "The Thought of the Outside," in *Essential Works of Foucault 1954–1984, Volume 2: Aesthetics, Method, and Epistemology* (New York: New, 1998), 147–70. The original publication date of the Foucault text is 1966. Deleuze and Guattari speak explicitly of a utopian place. See Gilles Deleuze and Félix Guattari, *Qu'est-ce que*

la philosophie? (Paris: Minuit, 1991), 95–96; English translation by Hugh Tomlinson and Graham Burchell as *What Is Philosophy?* (New York: Columbia University Press, 1994), 99–100. Deleuze and Guattari speak of the outside in *A Thousand Plateaus.* See Gilles Deleuze and Félix Guattari, *Mille plateaux* (Paris: Minuit, 1980), 34; English translation by Brian Massumi as *A Thousand Plateaus* (Minneapolis: University of Minnesota Press, 1987), 23. For the outside, see especially Gilles Deleuze, *Foucault* (Paris: Minuit, 1986); English translation by Seán Hand as *Foucault* (Minneapolis: University of Minnesota Press, 1988). The outside in Derrida anticipates his idea of a democracy to come. See Jacques Derrida, *Spectres de Marx* (Paris: Galilée, 1993), 143; English translation by Peggy Kamuf as *Specters of Marx* (New York: Routledge, 1994), 87.

7. In "Letter to a Japanese Friend," Derrida explains how he came to this word "deconstruction." See Jacques Derrida, "Lettre à un ami japonais (1985)," in *Psyché: Inventions de l'autre* (Paris: Galilée, 1987), 387–93; English translation by David Wood and Andrew Benjamin as "Letter to a Japanese Friend," in *Psyche: Inventions of the Other, Volume II,* edited by Peggy Kamuf and Elizabeth Rottenberg (Stanford, Calif.: Stanford University Press, 2008), 1–6.

8. Other classical definitions of deconstruction can be found in Jacques Derrida, *Force de loi* (Paris: Galilée, 1994), 47–63; English translation by Mary Quintance as "The Force of Law," in *Deconstruction and the Possibility of Justice,* edited by Drucilla Cornell, Michael Rosenfeld, and David Gray Carlson (New York: Routledge, 1992), 21–29. Another definition (much later) can be found in the essay "Et cetera," translated by Geoffrey Bennington in *Deconstructions: A User's Guide,* edited by Nicholas Royle (London: Palgrave, 2000), 300. Because Derrida's concept of deconstruction is so dependent on that of Heidegger, it is perhaps possible to think that Derrida's 1987 *Of Spirit* is the most important text on what deconstruction is. See Jacques Derrida, *De l'esprit* (Paris: Galilée, 1987); English translation by Geoffrey Bennington and Rachel Bowlby as *Of Spirit* (Chicago: University of Chicago Press, 1989).

9. Derrida also says that the oppositions are "violent." The first phase of deconstruction therefore participates in Derrida's long discourse on violence, which begins in 1964 with "Violence and Metaphysics" ("Violence et métaphysique," in *L'écriture et la différence,* 117–228; "Violence and Metaphysics," in *Writing and Difference,* 79–152), continues through "Force of Law," part 2 (which concerns Walter Benjamin's "Critique of Violence"), and finishes with *The Animal That Therefore I Am* (Jacques Derrida, *L'animal que donc je suis* [Paris: Galilée, 2006]; English translation by David Wills as *The Animal That Therefore I Am* [Stanford, Calif.: Stanford University Press, 2008).

10. In his English translation of *Positions,* Alan Bass renders the word "écart" as "interval." See Jacques Derrida, *Positions* (Paris: Minuit, 1972), 57; English translation by Alan Bass as *Positions* (Chicago: University of Chicago Press, 1981), 42.

11. Derrida, *Positions,* 95; *Positions,* 71. See also 88 of this book.

12. Derrida, *Positions,* 57; *Positions,* 42, translation modified.

13. Concerning deconstruction and exiting the terrain of metaphysics, see Derrida's final comments in "The Ends of Man." Jacques Derrida, "La fin de

l'homme," in *Marges de la philosophie* (Paris: Minuit, 1972), 162–63; English trans-lation by Alan Bass as "The Ends of Man," in *Margins of Philosophy* (Chicago: University of Chicago Press, 1982), 135.

14. What is really being put to the test is Husserl's concept of language. Can the being of language be oriented by the value of presence? The sign in its indicating or pointing function, doesn't it make the function of expressing the self-presence of a meaning *problematic*? Now we can shift the emphasis in the sub-title: "An Introduction to the *Problem* of the Sign in Husserl's Phenomenology." Later in his career, Derrida will return to the word "problem" and distinguish it from aporia. See Jacques Derrida, *Apories* (Paris: Galilée, 1996), 30–31; English translation by Thomas Dutoit as *Aporias* (Stanford, Calif.: Stanford University Press, 1993), 11–12.

15. Evidence of Husserl making the sign derivative can be found in his "principle of all principles," which Derrida cites (51); this principle instructs us to accept as evidence only what is intuitively—not semiotically—given. Evidence of Western metaphysics in general making the sign derivative can be found in Plato's *Phaedrus*, as Derrida has shown in "La pharmacie de Platon," in *La dissémination* (Paris: Seuil, 1972), 69–188; English translation by Barbara Johnson as "Plato's Pharmacy," in *Dissemination* (Chicago: University of Chicago Press, 1981), 61–171.

16. See Derrida, "Positions," in *Positions*, 74; "Positions," in *Positions*, 54–55 (my emphasis): "Wherever the *values* of propriety, of a proper meaning, of prox-imity to the self, of etymology, etc. imposed themselves in relation to the body, consciousness, language, writing, etc., I have attempted to analyze the meta-physical *desire* and presuppositions that were at work."

17. When Derrida is criticizing these ideas of desire and will, he is also criti-cizing Husserl's fundamental concept of intentionality. Instead of intentionality which is always directed to an object, Derrida is trying to conceive a movement which aims at a non-object. Aiming at a non-object means aiming at indetermi-nation or incompleteness, as in a question for which there is no absolute answer. Later in his career (as in *Specters of Marx*), Derrida will try to expand the idea of the question into that of the promise, and therefore his thinking will be messi-anic. But the messiah coming does not necessarily mean salvation since the mes-siah's coming cannot be calculated. The messiah might just as well be a threat. And since there is no beginning and end, the messiah never really comes in full presence. But Derrida is also reconceiving desire when he speaks of friend-ship and especially when he coins the term "aimance," which has been rendered in English as "lovence." See Jacques Derrida, *Politiques de l'amitié* (Paris: Galilée, 1994), 88; English translation by George Collins as *Politics of Friendship* (London: Verso Books, 1997), 69–70.

18. For a later use of the word "clôture" ("closure"), see Derrida, *Apories*, 79; *Aporias*, 40. The word "closure" still seems to be still invoked as late as Der-rida's 2003 *Rogues* when he speaks of the "tour," a circular image. See Jacques Derrida, *Voyous* (Paris: Galilée, 2003); English translation by Pascale-Anne Brault and Michael Naas as *Rogues* (Stanford, Calif.: Stanford University Press, 2005).

19. For the word "closure," see especially "'Genèse et structure' et la phé-noménologie," in *L'écriture et la différance*, 240–41; "'Genesis and Structure' and Phenomenology," in *Writing and Difference*, 162. Here Derrida cites Husserl, *Ideas I*, §72, where Husserl describes eidetic sciences. See also *De la grammatologie*, 25; *Of Grammatology*, 14.

20. See Jacques Derrida, "La forme et le vouloir-dire," in *Marges de la phi-losophie*, 185–207; *Margins of Philosophy*, 155–74.

21. See Derrida's 1988 interview with Jean-Luc Nancy for another dis-cussion of *Vergegenwärtigung*. Jacques Derrida, "Il faut bien manger," in *Points de suspension* (Paris: Galilée, 1992), 277–78; English translation by Peter Connor and Avital Ronnell as "Eating Well," in *Points . . . Interviews 1974–1994* (Stanford, Calif.: Stanford University Press, 1995), 263–64.

22. With the idea of a "beyond" (see 88), it is clear that Derrida is still engaged in some sort of meta-physical thinking. This "beyond" would not be another world, not something transcendent, but a "beyond" of this world. More-over, the idea of "beyond" implies that just as Derrida was able to reconceive the name "difference," he was able to reconceive the name "metaphysics." "Meta-physics" is a paleonym. If "metaphysics" is a paleonym, then Deleuze's comment about being a "pure metaphysician" does not seem alien to Derrida's thought. "Pure" here may mean a reconception of "beyond," not as something transcen-dent, but as the "beyond" of a line of flight. See Gilles Deleuze, "Responses to a Series of Questions," in *Collapse: Philosophical Research and Development* 3 (2007): 39–44.

23. See Jacques Derrida, "Différance," in *Marges de la philosophie*, 3–29; "Dif-férance," in *Margins of Philosophy*, 1–27.

24. The massive influence of Heidegger on Derrida's thought is clear. However throughout his career Derrida will attempt to find the schemas of the metaphysics of presence at work in Heidegger's thought (see 63 note vi). In short, Derrida engages in a lifelong debate with Heidegger. This debate begins with Derrida's 1968 essay "The Ends of Man," in *Margins of Philosophy*.

25. The book's title comes from chapter 6: "The phenomenon does not stop being an object for the voice. On the contrary . . . the ideality of the ob-ject seems to depend on the voice and thus becomes *absolutely available* in [the voice]" (67).

26. We can see that the entire movement of French thought of the 1960s bases itself on transcendental philosophy, if we look at two other books which belong to the same moment as Derrida's *Voice and Phenomenon:* Foucault's 1966 *The Order of Things*, whose project consists of determining "historical a priori"; and Deleuze's 1968 *Difference and Repetition*, whose project consists of deter-mining a "transcendental empiricism." See Gilles Deleuze, *Différence et répétition* (Paris: Presses Universitaires de France, 1968), 192; English translation by Paul Patton as *Difference and Repetition* (New York: Columbia University Press, 1994), 147; Michel Foucault, *Les mots et les choses* (Paris: Tel Gallimard, 1966), 170–71; anonymous English translation as *The Order of Things* (New York: Vintage, 1994), 157–58.

27. Because the old names are determined by the oppositions and hierarchies under deconstruction, Derrida has investigated negative theology and he has made use of the Platonic name "khôra." See Jacques Derrida, "Comment ne pas parler, Dénégations" (1986), in *Psyché: Inventions de l'autre* (Paris: Galilée, 1987), 535–95; English translation by Ken Frieden and Elizabeth Rottenberg as "How to Avoid Speaking: Denials," in *Psyche: Inventions of the Other, Volume II,* 143–94. See also Jacques Derrida, *Sauf le nom* (Paris: Galilée, 1993); English translation by John P. Leavey, Jr., as "Sauf le nom," in *On the Name,* edited by Thomas Dutoit (Stanford, Calif.: Stanford University Press, 1995), 35–87. Jacques Derrida, *Khôra* (Paris: Galilée, 1993); English translation by Ian McLeod as "Khôra," in *On the Name,* edited by Thomas Dutoit (Stanford, Calif.: Stanford University Press, 1995), 89–129.

28. See *Force de loi,* 35; "Force of Law," in *Deconstruction and the Possibility of Justice,* 15.

29. This claim must be made, even though Derrida is reconceiving what truth means. For Derrida, the truth consists of a structure or law which can never be made fully present, which can never be fully unveiled. The truth of truth for Derrida is the fact that there is no full presence. That there is no full presence means that truth as presence never appears as such, independently of falsehood or non-presence. For Derrida, falsehood in this sense is the truth of truth. See Jacques Derrida, *Éperons: Les styles de Nietzsche* (Paris: Champs Flammarion, 1978), 92–93; English translation by Barbara Harlow as *Spurs: Nietzsche's Styles* (Chicago: University of Chicago Press, 1979), 111.

30. For the role of hearing in deconstruction, and interior monologue in Heidegger, see Jacques Derrida, "L'oreille de Heidegger: Philopolémologie (Geschlecht IV)," in *Politiques de l'amitié,* 358; English translation by John P. Leavey, Jr., as "Heidegger's Ear: Philopolemology (Geschlecht IV)," in *Reading Heidegger: Commemorations,* edited by John Sallis (Bloomington: Indiana University Press), 175.

31. For undecidability, see Jacques Derrida, "La double séance," in *La dissémination,* 248–51; "The Double Session," in *Dissemination,* 219–21. The experience of undecidability can also be understood as the experience of responsibility. We see the theme of responsibility in Derrida as early as his 1962 translation of Husserl's "Origin of Geometry" (Edmund Husserl, *L'origine de la géométrie,* 166; *Edmund Husserl's "Origin of Geometry": An Introduction,* 149) and as late as his 1992 *Aporias* (Derrida, *Apories,* 40–42; *Aporias,* 18–19).

Introduction

1. Derrida is citing Suzanne Bachelard's French translation from 1957, *Logique formelle et Logique transcendentale,* §35b, p. 137.

2. Derrida had translated the fragment from *The Crisis* period called "The Origin of Geometry" into French in 1962; see the bibliography for the English translation by John P. Leavey, Jr.

3. Derrida never wrote this general interpretation, although throughout his career he alluded to, cited, or explicitly discussed Husserl, especially *The Crisis* and its associated texts. The English title of the First Logical Investigation is "Expression and Meaning."

4. The text to which Derrida is referring is from page 183 of the English translation of the *Logical Investigations;* Findley renders "Doppelsinn" as "ambiguity." Derrida will cite the French translation completed in 1963 by Hubert Elie, Arion L. Kelkel, and René Schérer. Throughout, all references to Husserl's *Logical Investigations* are to the revised Moran edition: Edmund Husserl, *Logical Investigations,* two volumes, translated by J. N. Findlay, with a new preface by Michael Dummett and edited with a new introduction by Dermot Moran (London: Routledge, 2001).

5. Derrida renders "Anzeichen" by "indice," which also means "index" like a personal pronoun. The personal pronoun "I" will be at the center of chapter 7. See "Translator's Note," point 10.

6. Derrida is citing the final pages of Husserl's introduction to volume 2 of the *Logical Investigations,* pages 21–22 of the German edition (which is contained in the English translation, volume 1, pages 178–79).

7. This text is published in Greek. There is an English translation. See Jacques Derrida, "Phenomenology and Metaphysical Closure," translated by F. Joseph Smith, in *Philosophy Today* 11, no. 2 (Summer 1967): 106–23. There is an updated English translation by Ronald Bruzina, in *The New Yearbook of Phenomenology 3* (Seattle: Noesis, 2003), 102–20. Bruzina has made this translation from Derrida's French version.

8. Derrida cites only §60 of the *Cartesian Meditations.* He lists no French edition or translators. But the quote is identical to the French translation produced by Gabrielle Pfeiffer and Emmanuel Levinas in 1947. This passage is from pages 223–24 of the French edition; the equivalent passage can be found on page 139 of the English translation.

9. Here Derrida is alluding to the ontological distinctions that Husserl makes in *Ideas I* (§96–97) between "real" in the sense of something factual, "reelle" (here Derrida uses the French word "réelle") in the sense of a part of consciousness, and "irreelle" (here Derrida uses the French word "irréelle") in the sense of something ideal but not factual and not a part of consciousness. See "Translator's Note," point 4, for a more detailed explanation of these differences.

10. Derrida cites simply "Preparatory Considerations, §2." The comment that he seems to have in mind is from page 21 of the English translation of *Formal and Transcendental Logic.*

11. Derrida cites p. 136 of the second volume of the French translation of the *Logical Investigations.* One can find this passage in volume 2 of the English translation on page 75. Here Derrida also says, "Each time that we shall cite this translation, we shall indicate this by the signs 'tr. fr.'" He then goes on to say that he has replaced in the French translation the word "significations" by "*Bedeutungen.*" This comment implies that when Derrida does not use the sign "tr. fr.," he is not using the available translation and instead is translating the *Logical Investigations* himself into French. See "Translator's Note," point 5.

12. This is Derrida's first thematic use of the Freudian term "instance," here rendered as "court of appeal." See "Translator's Note," point 8.

13. The French term being rendered as "hearth fire" is "foyer." The term is normally rendered in English as "focal point." But here Derrida is using the term to suggest the image of light. See also Jacques Derrida, *Positions* (Paris: Minuit, 1972), 55; English translation by Alan Bass as *Positions* (Chicago: University of Chicago Press, 1981), 40. See especially Alan Bass's translator's note 6 on p. 100 (for p. 40). The hearth (*foyer*) appears later in Derrida's work. See Jacques Derrida, *De l'esprit* (Paris: Galilée, 1987), 162; English translation by Geoffrey Bennington and Rachel Bowlby as *Of Spirit* (Chicago: University of Chicago Press, 1989), 99.

14. Derrida uses the French personal pronoun "le 'Je' " (in uppercase), which I have rendered as "the 'I' "; "le moi" as "the me"; and the Latin "ego" as "ego."

15. Derrida cites the Husserliana volume of *Phänomenologische Psychologie*, Husserliana volume IX, p. 342. The English translation of the volume does not contain the passage.

16. Derrida is alluding to one of Rimbaud's "Letters of a Visionary" (letter of 15 May 1871 to Paul Demeny): "Je est un autre."

17. This allusion is to the passage in the Fifth Meditation, on page 99 of the English translation. Cairns translates the German phrase as "mundanizing self-apperception."

18. Again Derrida is referring to the passage in the Fifth Cartesian Meditation, page 131 of the English translation.

19. Here Derrida cites Ricoeur's French translation of *Ideen I*, that is, *Idées I*, p. 182, which is §54. We have followed Ricoeur's translation here in the English. The equivalent passage is from page 127 of the Kersten English translation of *Ideas I*.

20. Derrida provides no citation for this quote. An English translation of the "Nachwort" can be found in *Husserl: Shorter Works*. Apparently Derrida is referring to comments that one can find in the English translation on pages 45 and 46. The equivalent passages may be found in §3 of the "Nachwort" collected in *Ideen III*, pages 144–48. The pages in the English *Cartesian Meditations* seem to be page 32 and page 131.

21. Derrida cites "Nachwort," p. 557. The equivalent passage is from page 46 of the Nachwort's English translation called "Author's Preface to the English Edition of Ideas," in *Husserl: Shorter Works;* here "Nuancierung" is rendered as "change in the shading." See "Nachwort" in *Ideen III*, p. 148.

22. Derrida's word here is "une prise." See "Translator's Note," point 14.

Chapter 1

1. The established French translation of Husserl's "Bedeutung" is "signification"; the standard English translation is "meaning." Derrida says that in German one can say that a *Zeichen* is deprived of *Bedeutung*, but "on ne peut dire en français, sans contradiction, qu'un sign est privé de signification." As in German, in English it is not a contradiction to say that a sign has no meaning since such

a sign (lacking, let us say, a conceptual meaning) may still indicate something or make a reference. But an Anglophone speaker would, it seems, never say that a sign signifies (that is, refers to) nothing; if it indicates nothing, the sign would no longer be a sign. Here English seems to overlap more with French. Derrida's point in the next few sentences is that a Francophone speaker would never speak of a sign that signifies nothing ("des signes non signifiants") because such a sign or thing would not be a sign, while in German one may speak of a *bedeutunglose Zeichen;* such a sign would be an indicative sign since it lacks only a conceptual meaning while still referring to something. For instance, appropriating Husserl's example of an indicative sign, one may say that the canals on Mars that are visible through a telescope indicate or refer to something (ancient rainfall, perhaps, or ancient Martian civilization), but the Martian canals lack the conceptual meaning that a sign such as a triangle contains.

2. This is the first time in the book that Derrida contrasts *de facto* (*en fait*) with *de jure* (*en droit*), when he speaks of "the right <*du droit*> to expression."

3. Derrida is suggesting that we can translate the verb "bedeuten" into French as "vouloir dire," which in English means literally "to want to say," or more normally, "to mean." Then the noun "Bedeutung" can be rendered in French as "vouloir-dire," "wanting-to-say," or "meaning." See "Translator's Note," point 11.

4. Between parentheses at the end of the quotation, Derrida refers to *Logical Investigations,* §15. There is no footnote that elaborates on the reference. The equivalent passage can be found in the English translation, volume 1, page 201. Derrida does not translate into French the terms "Bedeutung" and "Sinn," and he highlights the German word "gleichbedeutend."

5. Between parentheses at the end of the quote (without any footnote), Derrida refers to *Idées I,* §124. The equivalent passage can be found on page 294 of the Kersten English translation; Kersten renders "bedeuten" as "signifying," "Bedeutung" as "signification," and "Sinn" as "sense." In the quote, Derrida modifies Ricoeur's French translation of "bedeuten," substituting "vouloir-dire" for Ricoeur's "signifier." In this case, we have rendered "vouloir-dire" as "to want to say." Derrida does not translate into French the numerous occurrences of "Bedeutung" in the quotation; we have done the same in the English. Derrida also renders "verflochten" as "entrelacé," while Ricoeur renders it as "combiné."

6. Here, Derrida refers to *Idées I,* §124, between parentheses at the end of the quotation. The equivalent passage is from page 295 of the Kersten English translation.

7. Here, Derrida refers to the First Logical Investigation, §1, between parentheses at the end of the quotation; the equivalent passage can be found on page 183 of the English translation, volume 1.

8. Here, Derrida refers to First Logical Investigation, §1, between parentheses at the end of the quote; the equivalent passage can be found on page 183 of the English translation, volume 1. Findlay renders "Verflechtung" as "connection" and "verflochten" as "bound up with."

9. The equivalent passage can be found on page 183 of the English translation, volume 1; translation modified. Husserl's emphasis. Square brackets indicate Derrida's additions.

10. Here, Derrida refers to §1 between parentheses at the end of the quotation. The equivalent passage can be found on page 183 of the English translation, volume 1; the italics are Husserl's. Derrida's French translation is more faithful to Husserl's German, but Derrida mistakenly inserts the word "Bedeutungsintention" when the German says "Bedeutungsfunktion."

11. This is the first time Derrida has used the word "writing" (*écriture*).

Chapter 2

1. Derrida cites the passage to which he is referring in the next paragraph.

2. Here, Derrida refers to the First Logical Investigation, §2, between parentheses at the end of the quotation. The equivalent passage can be found on page 184 of the English translation, volume 1. Findlay renders "Überzeugung" as "belief" and "Vermutung" as "surmise"; he renders "Bestand" as "reality" and "Sein" as "reality." Derrida renders "Überzeugung" as "conviction" and "Vermutung" as "présomption," and I have rendered the two French terms literally as "conviction" and "presumption." Then Derrida renders "Bestand" as "consistence" and "Sein" as "être," which I have rendered respectively as "subsistence" and "being." The italics are Husserl's, which Derrida reproduces.

3. Derrida provides no reference for this quotation. It can be found in the First Logical Investigation, §3; the equivalent passage can be found on page 185 of the English translation, volume 1. The English translation omits Husserl's quotation marks around the word "form"; they are present in the French translation and reproduced here. "Indicative allusion" (*allusion indicative*) renders "Hinweis," which in the English translation is simply "indication" (as in the English translation of the title to §3), while "demonstration" (*démonstration*) renders "Beweis."

4. The term "monstration," which we have rendered in English with the same word, derives from the Latin "monstrare," which means "to show." The Latin verb is the root of the French verb "montrer," again, "to show." The phrase "points the finger" translates the French "montrer du doigt." Derrida is trying to get to the root of the distinctions between *Hinweis* (pointing at or pointing to) and *Beweis* (de-monstration), which the word "Weisen" ("to point") represents. As showing, Derrida's use of the term "monstration" should make one think of Heidegger's definition of the phenomenon, in *Being and Time*, (§7a) as that which shows itself from itself (*sich zeigen, das, was sich zeigt*). Later, in his confrontation with Heidegger, especially concerning the hand, Derrida will return to the idea of monstration. See Jacques Derrida, "*Geschlecht* II: Heidegger's Hand," in *Psyche: Inventions of the Other, Volume II,* 32.

Chapter 3

1. Derrida is rendering "Bedeutung" as "vouloir-dire," that is, in English literally as "wanting-to-say." Findlay renders Husserl's "bedeutsame Zeichen" as

"meaningful signs" on page 187 of the English translation of the *Logical Investigations*. We are rendering "vouloir-dire" in the normal way as "meaning"; at times, however, we shall insert "vouloir-dire" in the translation to remind the reader that "meaning" loses the sense of voluntarism which "vouloir-dire" implies. See "Translator's Note," point 11.

2. Husserl's German is "einsamen Seelenleben," which Findlay, on page 278 of the English translation, renders as "solitary life." Derrida's French, which we are following, is "vie solitaire de l'âme."

3. Derrida is citing page 421 of Ricoeur's French translation of *Ideas I*. See page 296 of Kersten's English translation for the equivalent passage. The italics in the quote from §124 are those of Husserl. The Derrida essay from 1967 was later collected in *Marges de la philosophie*, pp. 186–207; this volume exists in English translation as *Margins of Philosophy;* the essay, "Form and Meaning: A Note on the Phenomenology of Language," is from pp. 155–73.

4. Derrida provides no reference for this quotation. See the First Logical Investigation, §5. The equivalent passage can be found on page 187 of the English translation, volume 1.

5. Derrida provides no reference for this citation. See the First Logical Investigation, §5. The equivalent passage can be found on pages 187–88 of the English translation, volume 1.

6. The equivalent passage can be found on page 188 of the English translation, volume 1.

7. Derrida provides no reference for this quotation. See the First Logical Investigation, §6. The equivalent passage can be found on page 188 of the English translation, volume 1.

8. The phrase "originally framed" is from page 189 of the English translation, volume 1.

9. Derrida provides no reference for this citation. See the First Logical Investigation, §7. The equivalent passage can be found on page 189 of the English translation, volume 1.

10. Derrida provides no reference for this quotation. See the First Logical Investigation, §7. The equivalent passage can be found on pages 189–90 of the English translation, volume 1.

11. Derrida provides no reference for this quotation. See the First Logical Investigation, §8. The equivalent passage can be found on page 190 of the English translation, volume 1.

12. Derrida provides no reference for this quotation. See the First Logical Investigation, §8. The equivalent passage can be found on page 191 of the English translation, volume 1. Square brackets indicate Derrida's addition.

13. Derrida provides no reference for this quotation. See the First Logical Investigation, §8. The equivalent passage can be found on page 190 of the English translation, volume 1.

14. Derrida provides no reference for this quotation. See the First Logical Investigation, §8. The equivalent passage can be found on page 190 of the English translation, volume 1. Findlay translates "Hinzeigen" as "to point to" and "Anzeigen" as "indication."

15. The equivalent passage can be found on pages 190–91 of the English translation, volume 1. Square brackets indicate Derrida's additions, and Derrida has put the German "Bedeutung" back into the body of the translation.

16. Here Derrida is referring to *Ideas I,* §70. See page 160 of Kersten's English translation of *Ideas I* for the equivalent passage.

17. Derrida provides no reference for this quotation. See the First Logical Investigation, §8. The equivalent passage can be found on page 191 of the English translation, volume 1. Square brackets indicate Derrida's additions.

18. In *Of Grammatology,* which is contemporaneous with *Voice and Phenomenon* (1967), Derrida discusses Saussure at length; see the entire chapter "Linguistics and Grammatology."

19. Derrida provides no reference for this quotation. See the First Logical Investigation, §8. The equivalent passage can be found on page 191 of the English translation, volume 1. Findlay does not render Husserl's "gar," which the French translation renders as "encore moins," "still less."

Chapter 4

1. Derrida provides no reference for this quotation. See the First Logical Investigation, §8. The equivalent passage can be found on page 191 of the English translation, volume 1. Square brackets indicate Derrida's additions. Derrida reproduces Husserl's emphasis of "speaks" (*spricht*), which Findlay's translation omits.

2. In the note to *Leçon pour une phénoménologie de la conscience intime du temps,* Henri Dussort writes (this is my translation from Dussort), "Vergegenwärtigung, term generally translated <into French> as 'présentification.' But rather than this clumsy neologism, we prefer to have recourse to a typographical artifice <Dussort is referring to the hyphen in 're-présentation,' an artifice that Derrida adopts here> (while reserving 'représentation' for the translation of *Vorstellung*). This current term in German (and the verb *vergegenwärtigen*) correspond in effect exactly to the French expression 'se représenter' (in thought). <It corresponds to representing something to oneself in thought or thinking about something.> In Husserl it is opposed to perception (see the Sixth Logical Investigation, §37: 'The intentional character of perception is, in opposition to the mere representation of imagination, direct presentation.' <The Husserl quotation is from page 260 of volume 2 of the English translation.>)" Dussort continues: "Moreover we will discover, several times, when the two terms *Repräsentation* and *Vergegenwärtigung* are used as equivalents." In regard to the French translation of the *Logical Investigations,* Derrida is referring to an appendix on how to translate Husserl's German terms into French. There is a one-page discussion of the terms *Vorstellung* and *Repräsentation*. The French translators distinguish the two terms by saying that *Vorstellung* is a representation in the sense of an idea or image and is immediately present to consciousness; they moreover suggest that this term is closer to "presentation." *Repräsentation,* they say, is a representation in the sense of a substitute or a placeholder, a representative; they add that it is still a rep-

resentation in the sense of a *Vorstellung* since it is present to consciousness. The French translators decided to render both by "représentation."

3. This is the first occurrence of the word "deconstruction" in *Voice and Phenomenon,* although the word "destruction" occurs in the introduction.

4. Derrida is citing his own introduction to his own French translation of "The Origin of Geometry." He cites pages 60–69, which are in §5 of the introduction. See *Edmund Husserl's "Origin of Geometry": An Introduction,* pp. 69–76. David Carr's English translation of "The Origin of Geometry" is also contained in this volume.

5. Here, Derrida refers to *Idées I,* §111, between parentheses at the end of the quotation. The equivalent passage can be found in *Ideas I* (Kersten translation), p. 260; these are Husserl's italics.

6. Here, Derrida refers to *Idées'I,* §111, between parentheses at the end of the quotation. The equivalent passage can be found in *Ideas I* (Kersten translation), p. 260; these are Husserl's italics.

7. Derrida provides no reference for this quotation. See the First Logical Investigation, §8. The equivalent passage can be found on page 191 of the English translation, volume 1. Square brackets indicate Derrida's additions.

8. Here, Derrida refers to *Idées I,* §111, between parentheses at the end of the quotation. The equivalent passage can be found in *Ideas I* (Kersten translation), p. 261.

9. Derrida provides no reference for this quotation. See the First Logical Investigation, §8. The equivalent passage can be found on page 191 of the English translation, volume 1.

Chapter 5

1. Derrida does not provide a reference for his claim about Heidegger.

2. Here, between parentheses at the end of the quotation, Derrida refers to the French translation of *Vorlesungen zur Phänomenologie des inneren Zeitbewusstsein,* that is, *Leçons pour une phénoménologie de la conscience intime du temps,* p. 65. The equivalent passage can be found in The *Phenomenology of Internal Time-Consciousness,* §19, p. 70.

3. Here, between parentheses at the end of the quotation, Derrida refers to the French translation of *Vorlesungen zur Phänomenologie des inneren Zeitbewusstsein,* that is, *Leçons pour une phénoménologie de la conscience intime du temps,* p. 42. The equivalent passage can be found in *The Phenomenology of Internal Time-Consciousness,* §10, pp. 48–49.

4. Here, between parentheses at the end of the quotation, Derrida refers to the French translation of *Vorlesungen zur Phänomenologie des inneren Zeitbewusstsein,* that is, *Leçons pour une phénoménologie de la conscience intime du temps,* p. 45. The equivalent passage can be found in *The Phenomenology of Internal Time-Consciousness,* §11, p. 52.

5. Here, between parentheses at the end of the quotation, Derrida refers to the French translation of *Vorlesungen zur Phänomenologie des inneren Zeit-*

bewusstsein, that is, *Leçons pour une phénoménologie de la conscience intime du temps,* p. 55. The equivalent passage can be found in *The Phenomenology of Internal Time-Consciousness,* §16, p. 61.

6. Here, Derrida refers to §81 of *Idées I* between parentheses at the end of the quotation. The equivalent passage can be found on page 195 of the Kersten translation of *Ideas I;* these are Husserl's italics.

7. Here, Derrida refers to §81 of *Idées I* between parentheses at the end of the quotation. The equivalent passage can be found on page 195 of the Kersten translation of *Ideas I;* this is Husserl's emphasis.

8. Here, between parentheses at the end of the quotation, Derrida refers to the French translation of *Vorlesungen zur Phänomenologie des inneren Zeitbewusstsein,* that is, *Leçons pour une phénoménologie de la conscience intime du temps,* p. 58, §17. The equivalent passage can be found on page 64 of *The Phenomenology of Internal Time-Consciousness;* the italics are Husserl's.

9. Here, between parentheses at the end of the quotation, Derrida has a simple "ibid." He is referring to *Leçons pour une phénoménologie de la conscience intime du temps,* 58, §17. The equivalent passage can be found on page 64 of *The Phenomenology of Internal Time-Consciousness.*

10. Derrida provides no reference for this quotation. The quotation can be found in *The Phenomenology of Internal Time-Consciousness,* §16, page 62. Derrida's emphasis.

11. Derrida provides no reference for this quotation. The quotation can be found in *The Phenomenology of Internal Time-Consciousness,* §16, page 63; the italics are Husserl's.

12. Here, between parentheses at the end of the quotation, Derrida refers to *Leçons pour une phénoménologie de la conscience intime du temps,* p. 98, §36. The reference is incorrect. The quotation in fact comes from §35. The equivalent passage can be found on page 99 of *The Phenomenology of Internal Time-Consciousness.*

13. This is the first occurrence in this book of Derrida's neologism "différance" and the first occurrence of the word "trace."

Chapter 6

1. Here, Derrida refers to chapter 3 between parentheses at the end of the quotation. He is referring to the First Logical Investigation, §26. The equivalent passage can be found on page 219 of the English translation, volume 1.

2. "Form and Meaning" is collected in *Margins of Philosophy.* Aside from "Form and Meaning," Derrida never produced this close study of these sections of *Ideas I.*

3. Derrida cites Suzanne Bachelard's French translation, *Logique formelle et logique transcendentale,* page 75. Bachelard, however, has rendered Husserl's German as "portant en soi aussitôt un nouveau principle pour des constructions de formes." The word "complication" does not appear in this section. Derrida's use of the term is perhaps an error. The passage to which Derrida is refer-

ring is from pages 52–53 of the English translation. Cairns also uses the word "construction."

4. Derrida provides no reference for this comment. He is apparently referring to Heidegger's *Introduction to Metaphysics,* chapter 2, "The Grammar and Etymology of 'Being,'" pages 55–78.

5. Derrida has the word "Wiederzuspiegeln." But this word appears to be a typographical error; the correct word is "Widerzuspiegeln." See also 27, where Derrida speaks of the same idea of mirror reflection.

6. The French adjective, "historial," here transliterated into English, is a neologism. It seems to indicate a sense of history that is prior to, as a condition of possibility, "the history of idealization, that is, the 'history of spirit' or history as such." In other words, history would not be possible without the essential role that the *phonē* plays, making possible repetition of the same, in idealization. This linguistic repetition in idealization should not be conceived as what Derrida here calls "the history of idealization," which refers to the different ways idealization has been conceived in history of metaphysics. In his earlier introduction to Husserl's "The Origin of Geometry," Derrida had investigated the role of language in idealization; see §7 of the introduction. The term "historial" appears later in Derrida's work. See *De l'esprit,* 164–65; *Of Spirit,* 100.

7. With the word "glossamatics," Derrida is referring to the work of the linguist Louis Hjelmslev. In the contemporaneous *Of Grammatology,* Derrida discusses Hjelmslev at length; see *Of Grammatology,* 57–61.

8. Derrida does not indicate a particular text or title. But one could examine his two main texts on Hegel, "The Pit and the Pyramid," collected in *Margins of Philosophy,* and *Glas.*

9. Derrida is citing his own introduction to his own French translation of "The Origin of Geometry." He cites pages 83–100, which is the beginning of §7. See *Edmund Husserl's "Origin of Geometry": An Introduction,* 87–99.

10. Derrida provides no reference here. See Heidegger, *Kant and the Problem of Metaphysics,* §34.

11. Here, between parentheses at the end of the quotation, Derrida refers to *Leçons,* supplément 1, p. 131. The equivalent passage can be found in *The Phenomenology of Internal Time-Consciousness,* appendix 1, p. 131.

Chapter 7

1. The quote is from the First Logical Investigation, §9. The equivalent passage can be found on pages 191–92 of the English translation, volume 1.

2. Derrida provides no reference for this quotation. It comes from the First Logical Investigation, §9. The equivalent passage can be found on page 192 of the English translation, volume 1.

3. Derrida is referring to §12 of *Formal and Transcendental Logic,* page 49 of Cairns's English translation. In the contemporaneous *Of Grammatology* (pp. 48–49), Derrida says, "As in Husserl (but the analogy, although it is most

thought-provoking, would stop there and one must apply it carefully), the lowest level, the foundation of the possibility of logic (or semiotics) corresponds to the project of the *Grammatica speculativa* of Thomas of Erfurt, falsely attributed to Duns Scotus. Like Husserl, Peirce expressly refers to it. It is a matter of elaborating, in both cases, a formal doctrine of conditions which a discourse must satisfy in order to have a sense, in order to 'want to say,' even if it is false or contradictory."

4. Derrida is referring to the First Logical Investigation, §15. He continues the discussion of non-sense expressions such as "vert est ou" ("Grün ist oder," "green is or") in his 1971 essay on Austin, "Signature, Event, Context," collected in *Margins of Philosophy;* see in particular pages 318–21.

5. Derrida is referring to the First Logical Investigation, §15. The equivalent passage can be found on page 203 of the English translation, volume 1. The German terms to which Derrida is referring can be found in the following sentence from page 56 of volume 2, part 1 of the German edition: "Der Wechsel gleichsam, der auf die Anschauung ausgestellt ist, wird eingelöst." Derrida renders "einlösen" as "honorer." The metaphor is that of cashing in a check drawn on a bank account.

6. The equivalent passage can be found on pages 199–200 of the English translation, volume 1.

7. Derrida provides no reference for this quotation. See the First Logical Investigation, §26. The equivalent passage can be found on page 218 of the English translation, volume 1.

8. Derrida provides no reference for this quotation. See the First Logical Investigation, §26. The equivalent passage can be found on page 218 of the English translation, volume 1.

9. Here Derrida cites the French translation, "tr. fr., p. 100." The equivalent passage can be found in the First Logical Investigation, §26, on page 220 of the English translation, volume 1.

10. Here the word "Gegenlosigskeit" appears as "Gegenlosikeit"; this misspelling is probably a printer's error.

11. This quote is the first epigraph for the book. It can be found in Husserl's *First Logical Investigation,* chapter 3, §26; the quote is located on page 82 of volume 2, part 1, of the German edition and pages 218–19 of volume 1 of the English translation.

12. This sentence alludes to the Edgar Allan Poe epigraph at the beginning of *Voice and Phenomenon:* "I have spoken both of 'sound' and 'voice.' I mean to say that the sound was one of distinct, of even wonderfully, thrillingly distinct, syllabification. M. Valdemar *spoke,* obviously in reply to the question. . . . He now said: 'Yes;—no;—*I have been sleeping*—and now—now—*I am dead*'." The Poe quote, which I have modified in order to make it consistent with Derrida's French, can be found in *The Unabridged Edgar Allan Poe* (Philadelphia: Running, 1983), on page 1070, Poe's italics. The title of the volume in which the French translation of this story can be found is *Histoires extraordinaires* (extraordinary stories), hence Derrida's phrase "extraordinary story" here. It is not clear which edition of *Histoires extraodinaires* Derrida was using, but both were translations

made by Charles Baudelaire. It is probable that Derrida was using the 1962 edition. See Edgar Allan Poe, *Histoires extraordinaires* (Paris: Éditions Garnier Frères, 1962), p. 226.

13. Within the text, Derrida cites §11. The equivalent passage can be found in the First Logical Investigation on page 196 of the English translation, volume 1.

14. The sentence is "Autrement dit, le vrai et authentique vouloir-dire est le vouloir dire-vrai." The "subtle shift" ("subtil déplacement") to which Derrida refers in the next sentence is the shift in the hyphen from "vouloir-dire" to "le vouloir dire-vrai," from meaning to a will to say-the-truth.

15. Here, Derrida refers to §28 between parentheses at the end of the quotation. In a footnote, Derrida then cites pages 106–7 of the French translation (tr. fr.) and says, "We have inserted the word 'Bedeutung' and added the emphasis to the two full sentences." The equivalent passage can be found in the First Logical Investigation on pages 223–24 of the English translation, volume 1.

16. Here the word "Gegenwärtigung" appears as "Gegenvärtigung"; this misspelling is probably a printer's error.

17. The passage comes from *Ideas I*, §100; the equivalent passage can be found on pages 246–47 of the Kersten English translation. This quotation is the second epigraph for *Voice and Phenomenon*. The quotation comes from *Ideas I*, chapter 4, §100. It can be found on page 211 of the German, page 246 of the Kersten translation, and page 350 of Ricoeur's French translation. Kersten's English translation has been modified in order to make it consistent with Derrida's French translation, which is that of Paul Ricoeur. Ricoeur had used "etc." to render Husserl's "und so weiter." The French word rendered as "wander" is "errons," and thus "wander" should be associated with errancy.

18. The French word rendered by "comprehended" is "comprise," which is the past participle of "comprendre," a word connected to "prendre," the primary verb Derrida uses here to connote contamination. The word "comprendre" is the French word for "to understand," "to comprehend," and "to include."

19. Derrida italicizes "case" (*cas*) because Husserl, in *Ideas I*, §100, calls the description of the gallery "such a complicated case" (*so sehr komplizierter Fälle*). Ricoeur renders this as "d'exemple si compliqué" (p. 350), and Kersten renders it as "such very complicated examples" (p. 247). Here Derrida's wording is closer to Husserl's German.

20. Here when Derrida says "a little later," he is referring to *Ideas I*, §101, where Husserl again speaks of the Dresden gallery example or "case." There Husserl says, "Im obigen Beispiele: Der Blick kann in der Stufe Dresdner Galerie bleiben." Ricoeur renders this sentence as "Pour reprendre l'exemple ci-dessus, le regard peut s'arrêter au degré: gallerie de Dresde" (p. 352). Kersten renders this sentence as "In the previous example: the regard can remain at the level of the Dresden Gallery" (p. 248). Unlike Ricoeur, Derrida is rendering Husserl's "bleiben" as "demeurer." So here, following Kersten's English-language rendering, we have used "remain" to render "demeurer." Throughout, we have rendered "regard" (the French translation of Husserl's "Blick") as "look" (and not as "regard" as Kersten renders "Blick" here)."

Bibliography

Books by Edmund Husserl

Husserliana volumes

Hua I: *Cartesianische Meditationen und Pariser Vortrage,* edited by S. Strasser. The Hague: Martinus Nijhoff, 1963. 2nd edition. English translation by Dorian Cairns as *Cartesian Meditations.* The Hague: Martinus Nijhoff, 1960. French translation by Gabrielle Pfeiffer and Emmanuel Levinas as *Méditations Cartésiennes.* Paris: Vrin, 1992.

Hua II: *Die Idee der Phänomenologie,* edited by Walter Biemel. The Hague: Martinus Nijhoff, 1958. English translation by William P. Alston and George Nakhnikian as *The Idea of Phenomenology.* The Hague: Martinus Nijhoff, 1964.

Hua III.1: *Ideen zu einer reinen Phänomenologie und phanomenologischen Philosophie: Erstes Buch,* edited by Karl Schuhmann. The Hague: Martinus Nijhoff, 1976. English translation by F. Kersten as *Ideas Pertaining to a Pure Phenomenology and to a Phenomenological Philosophy.* The Hague: Martinus Nijhoff, 1982.

Hua III.2: *Ideen zu einer reinen Phänomenologie und phanomenologischen Philosophie: Erganzende Texte (1912–1929),* edited by Karl Schuhmann. The Hague: Martinus Nijhoff, 1976. English translation by Richard Rojcewicz and André Schuwer as *Ideas Pertaining to a Pure Phenomenology and to a Phenomenological Philosophy: Second Book: Studies in the Phenomenology of Constitution.* Dordrecht: Kluwer Academic, 1989.

Hua V: *Ideen zu einer reinen Phänomenologie und phanomenologischen Philosophie: Drittes Buch,* edited by Marly Biemel. The Hague: Martinus Nijhoff, 1952. English translation by Ted E. Kelin and William E. Pohl as *Phenomenology and the Foundation of the Sciences: Third Book: Ideas Pertaining to a Pure Phenomenology and to a Phenomenological Philosophy.* The Hague: Martinus Nijhof, 1980. Hua V contains the "Nachwort" to *Ideas I,* but the English translation does not contain it. The English translation of the "Nachwort" can be found in *Husserl: Shorter Works;* see below.

Hua VI: *Die Krisis der Europaischen Wissenschaften und die transzendentale Phänomenologie.* The Hague: Martinus Nijhoff, 1962. English translation by David Carr as *The Crisis of European Sciences and Transcendental Phenomenology.* Evanston, Ill.: Northwestern University Press, 1970.

Hua IX: *Phänomenologische Psychologie,* edited by Walter Biemel. The Hague: Martinus Nijhoff, 1966. Partial English translation by John Scanlon as *Phenomenological Psychology.* The Hague: Martinus Nijhoff, 1977.
Hua X: *Zur Phänomenologie des inneren Zeitbewusstseins (1893–1917),* edited by Rudolf Boehm. The Hague: Martinus Nijhoff, 1966. English translation by John Brough as *The Phenomenology of the Consciousness of Internal Time.* The Hague: Martinus Nijhoff, 1990.
Hua XVII: *Formal und Transzendentale Logik,* edited by Paul Janssen. The Hague: Martinus Nijhoff, 1974. English translation by Dorian Cairns as *Formal and Transcendental Logic.* The Hague: Martinus Nijhoff, 1978. French translation by Suzanne Bachelard as *Logique formelle et logique transcendentale.* Paris: Presses Universitaires de France, 1957.

Other Books by Edmund Husserl

Idées directrices pour une phénoménologie, trans. Paul Ricoeur. Paris: Gallimard, 1950.
Logische Unterschungen, two volumes, with volume 2 having two parts. Tubingen: Niemeyer, 1980. English translation by J. N. Findlay as *Logical Investigations,* two volumes. With a new preface by Michael Dummett and edited with a new introduction by Dermot Moran. London: Routledge Taylor and Francis, 2001. French translation by Hubert Elie, Arion L. Kelkel, and René Schérer as *Recherches logiques,* in three volumes. Paris: Presses Universitaires de France, 1959–63.
Erfahrung und Urteil, ed. Ludwig Landgrebe. Hamburg: Classen, 1938. English translation by James Churchill and Karl Ameriks as *Experience and Judgment.* Evanston, Ill.: Northwestern University Press, 1973.
Husserl: Shorter Works, ed. Peter McCormick and Frederick Elliston. Notre Dame, Ind.: Notre Dame University Press, 1981.
Vorlesungen zur Phänomenologie des inneren Zeitbewusstsein, ed. Martin Heidegger. Halle: Max Niemeyer, 1928. English translation by James Churchill as *The Phenomenology of Internal Time-Consciousness.* The Hague: Martinus Nijhoff, 1964. French translation by Henri Dussort as *Leçons pour une phénoménologie de la conscience intime du temps.* Paris: Presses Universitaires de France, 1964.

Books and Articles by Jacques Derrida

L'animal que donc je suis. Paris: Galilée, 2006. English translation by David Wills as *The Animal That Therefore I Am.* Stanford, Calif.: Stanford University Press, 2008.
Apories. Paris: Galilée, 1996. English translation by Thomas Dutoit as *Aporias.* Stanford, Calif.: Stanford University Press, 1993.
La dissémination. Paris: Seuil, 1972. English translation by Barbara Johnson as *Dissemination.* Chicago: University of Chicago Press, 1981.

BIBLIOGRAPHY

Du droit à la philosophie. Paris: Galilée, 1990. English translation by Jan Plug and others as *Eyes of the University: Right to Philosophy 2.* Stanford, Calif.: Stanford University Press, 2004.

L'ecriture et la différence. Paris: Seuil, 1967. English translation by Alan Bass as *Writing and Difference.* Chicago: University of Chicago, 1978.

Éperons: Les styles de Nietzsche. Paris: Champs Flammarion, 1978. English translation by Barbara Harmow as *Spurs: Nietzsche's Styles.* Chicago: University of Chicago Press, 1979.

De l'esprit. Paris: Galilée, 1987. English translation by Geoffrey Bennington and Rachel Bowlby as *Of Spirit.* Chicago: University of Chicago Press, 1989.

"Et cetera," translated by Geoffrey Bennington, in *Deconstructions: A User's Guide,* edited by Nicholas Royle. London: Palgrave, 2000, pp. 282–305.

Force de loi. Paris: Galilée, 1994. English translation by Mary Quintance as "The Force of Law," in *Deconstruction and the Possibility of Justice,* edited by Drucilla Cornell, Michael Rosenfeld, and David Gray Carlson. New York: Routledge, 1992. 21–29.

Glas. Paris: Denoël/Gontheier, 1981 [1974], two volumes. English translation by John P. Leavey, Jr., and Richard Rand as *Glas.* Lincoln: University of Nebraska Press, 1986.

De la grammatologie. Paris: Minuit, 1967. English translation by Gayatri Spivak as *Of Grammatology.* Baltimore: Johns Hopkins University Press, 1997, corrected edition.

"Il faut bien manger," in *Points de Suspension.* Paris: Galilée, 1992, pp. 269–301. English translation by Peter Connor and Avital Ronnell as "Eating Well," in *Points . . . Interviews 1974–1994.* Stanford: Stanford University Press, 1995, pp. 255–87.

Khôra. Paris: Galilée, 1993. English translation by Ian McLeod as "Khôra," in *On the Name,* edited by Thomas Dutoit. Stanford, Calif.: Stanford University Press, 1995, 89–129.

"La main de Heidegger (*Geschlecht* II) (1984–1985)." In *Psyché.* Paris: Galilée, 1987, 415–52. English translation by John P. Leavey, Jr., and Elizabeth Rottenberg as "*Geschlecht* II: Heidegger's Hand," in *Psyche: Inventions of the Other, Volume II,* edited by Peggy Kamuf and Elizabeth Rottenberg. Stanford, Calif.: Stanford University Press, 2008, 27–62.

Marges de la philosophie. Paris: Minuit, 1972. English translation by Alan Bass as *Margins of Philosophy.* Chicago: University of Chicago Press, 1982.

"L'oreille de Heidegger: Philopolémologie (Geschlecht IV)." In *Politiques de l'amitié.* Paris: Galilée, 1994, 343–419. English translation by John P. Leavey, Jr., as "Heidegger's Ear: Philopolemology (Geschlecht IV)," in *Reading Heidegger: Commemorations,* edited by John Sallis. Bloomington: Indiana University Press, 163–219.

[Husserl, Edmund.] *L'origine de la géométrie, traduction et introduction par Jacques Derrida.* Paris: Presses Universitaires de France, 1974 [1962]. English translation by John P. Leavey, Jr., as *Edmund Husserl's "Origin of Geometry": An Introduction.* Lincoln: University of Nebraska Press, 1989 [1978].

"La phénoménologie et la cloture de la métaphysique." In *EΠOXEΣ*, Athens, February 1966. English translation by F. Joseph Smith as "Phenomenology and Metaphysical Closure," in *Philosophy Today* 11, no. 2 (Summer 1967): 106–23. English translation by Ronald Bruzina, in *The New Yearbook of Phenomenology 3* (Seattle, Noesis, 2003): 102–20. Bruzina has made this translation from Derrida's French version.

Politiques de l'amitié. Paris: Galilée, 1994. English translation by George Collins as *Politics of Friendship.* London: Verso Books, 1997.

Positions. Paris: Minuit, 1972. English translation by Alan Bass as *Positions.* Chicago: University of Chicago Press, 1981

Le problem de la genèse dans la philosophie de Husserl. Paris: Presses Universitaires de France, 1990. English translation by Marian Hobson as *The Problem of Genesis in Husserl's Philosophy.* Chicago: University of Chicago Press, 2003.

Psyché: Inventions de l'autre. Paris: Galilée, 1987. English translation edited by Peggy Kamuf and Elizabeth Rottenberg as *Psyche: Inventions of the Other, Volume II.* Stanford, Calif.: Stanford University Press, 2008.

Sauf le nom. Paris: Galilée, 1993. English translation by John P. Leavey, Jr., as "Sauf le nom," in *On the Name,* edited by Thomas Dutoit. Stanford, Calif.: Stanford University Press, 1995, 35–87.

Spectres de Marx. Paris: Galilée, 1993. English translation by Peggy Kamuf as *Specters of Marx.* New York: Routledge, 1994.

Le toucher—Jean-Luc Nancy. Paris: Galilée, 2000. English translation by Christine Irizarry as *On Touching—Jean-Luc Nancy.* Stanford, Calif.: Stanford University Press, 2005.

Voyous. Paris: Galilée, 2003. English translation by Pascale-Anne Brault and Michael Naas as *Rogues.* Stanford, Calif.: Stanford University Press, 2005.

Books by Other Authors

Deleuze, Gilles. *Différence et répétititon.* Paris: Presses Universitaires de France, 1968. English translation by Paul Patton as *Difference and Repetition.* New York: Columbia University Press, 1994.

———. *Foucault.* Paris: Minuit, 1986. English translation by Seán Hand as *Foucault.* Minneapolis: University of Minnesota Press, 1988.

———. "Responses to a Series of Questions." In *Collapse: Philosophical Research and Development* 3 (2007): 39–44.

Deleuze, Gilles, and Félix Guattari. *Mille plateaux.* Paris: Minuit, 1980. English translation by Brian Massumi as *A Thousand Plateaus.* Minneapolis: University of Minnesota Press, 1987.

———. *Qu'est-ce que la philosophie?* Paris: Minuit, 1991. English translation by Hugh Tomlinson and Graham Burchell as *What Is Philosophy?* New York: Columbia University Press, 1994.

Foucault, Michel. *Les mots et les choses.* Paris: Tel Gallimard, 1966. Anonymous English translation as *The Order of Things.* New York: Vintage, 1994.

————. "La pensée du dehors." In *Dits et écrits I 1954–1975*. Paris: Quarto Gallimard, 2001, 546–67. English translation by Brian Massumi as "The Thought of the Outside," in *Essential Works of Foucault 1954–1984: Volume 2: Aesthetics, Method, and Epistemology*. New York: New, 1998, 147–70.

Freud, Sigmund. *The Complete Psychological Works of Sigmund Freud, Volume XII (1911–1913), The Case of Schreber*. London: Hogarth, 1958.

Heidegger, Martin. *Einführung in die Metaphysik*. Tübingen: Max Niemeyer Verlag, 1987. English translation by Gregory Fried and Richard Polt as *Introduction to Metaphysics*. New Haven, Conn.: Yale University Press, 2000.

————. *Kant und das Problem der Metaphysik*. Frankfurt am Main: Klostermann, 1973. English translation by Richard Taft as *Kant and the Problem of Metaphysics*, 4th edition, enlarged. Bloomington: Indiana University Press, 1990.

————. *Sein und Zeit*. Tübingen: Max Niemeyer Verlag, 1979. English translation by Joan Stambaugh as *Being and Time*, revised and with a foreword by Dennis J. Schmidt. Albany: SUNY Press, 2010.

Hjelmslev, Louis. *Outline of Glossematics: A Study in the Methodology of the Humanities with Special Reference to Linguistics (Travaux du Cercle linguistique de Copenhague)*. Copenhagen: Nordisk sprog- og kulturforlag, 1957.

Lacan, Jacques. *Écrits*. Paris: Seuil, 1966. English translation by Bruce Fink as *Écrits: The First Complete Edition in English*. New York: Norton, 2007.

Laplanche, Jean, and Jean-Bertrand Pontalis. *Vocabulaire de la psychanalyse*. Paris: Presses Universitaires de France, 1967. English translation by Donad Nicholson-Smith as *The Language of Psychoanalysis*. New York: W.W. Norton, 1973.

Poe, Edgar Allan. *Histoires extraordinaires*. Paris: Garnier, 1962.

————. *The Unabridged Edgar Allan Poe*. Philadelphia: Running, 1983.

Saussure, Ferdinand de. *Cours de linguistique générale*. Paris: Payot, 1916. English translation by Roy Harris as *Course in General Linguistics*. Open Court, 1998.

Index

The selection of page numbers for frequently appearing terms such as *expression, indication, discourse, language, sign, signification, meaning, sense,* and *presence* has been guided by the apparent importance of what Derrida says at that point in the commentary. Likewise, separate entries have been formed for variants of a term when it seems as though Derrida's commentary is distinguishing them (for instance, between *expression* and *expressivity, representation* and *representivity,* and especially between *sign, signifier, signified,* and *signification*). Other terms have been combined under the main invariant (for instance, *norm* and *abnormal* are both found under the term *normalcy*).

41, 42, 43, 48, 49, 50, 59, 60, 62, 76, 81n, 82

comparison, xx, 3n†, 55

complexity, xxii, 13, 14, 16, 17, 31, 35, 37n, 39n, 53, 75, 86; complex, complicity, 38n, 64, 66; complicated, xiv, 49; complication, 63, 75, 103n3, 106n19. *See also* fold; simplicity

concept, xi, xii, xiii, xiv, xv, xvi, xvii, xix, xxiii, xxv, xxvi, 3, 6, 7, 9, 11, 12, 13, 14, 15, 16, 17, 18, 19, 20, 21, 22, 24, 25, 26, 28, 29, 31, 32, 33, 36, 38, 39, 40, 43, 44, 47, 50, 52, 53, 54n*, 59, 63, 63n†, 64, 66, 68, 70, 71, 72, 72n, 73, 75, 76, 80, 81n, 84, 85, 86, 87, 88, 92n8, 93n14, 93n17, 94n22, 98n1

confession (*avouer, aveu*), xxviii, 15, 47

Connor, Peter, 94n21

consciousness (*conscience*), xiv, xix, xx, xxix, 8, 9, 10, 11, 12, 13, 14, 19, 27, 28, 29, 33, 34, 37, 38n, 39, 40, 49, 50, 53, 54, 54n†, 56, 57n, 58, 58n*, 65, 66, 68, 75, 78n, 84, 87, 88, 93n16, 96n9, 101n2; preconscious, 30

constitution, xviii, xx, xxiv, 3n†, 4, 6, 7, 10, 13, 14, 21, 22, 26, 28, 36, 38n, 42, 43, 44, 45, 46n, 52, 55, 56, 57, 58, 59, 60, 65, 69, 70, 71, 72n, 73, 74, 77, 78n, 82, 83, 87

contamination (*see* xxxii #14), xv, xxv, xxviii, 17, 19, 61, 80, 106n18. *See also* grip (*prendre*)

content, xvi, xvii, xxii, xxv, 6, 16, 18, 19, 21, 25, 27, 34, 36, 38, 38n, 40, 46, 51n, 53, 54, 57n, 79, 79n, 80, 83, 84, 85, 86. *See also* matter

context, 80

contingent (*eventuellement; see* xxxiii #21), xviii, 4, 25, 42, 46, 48, 49, 55, 74, 77, 80, 83

continuity, xxi, 53, 56, 57, 72n. *See also* discontinuity

contradiction, xvii, 7, 13, 15, 26, 46n, 49n, 58, 61, 67, 74, 76, 78, 82, 97n1, 105n3

Cornell, Drucilla, 92n8

crisis, 70

critique, xi, xii, 4, 5, 6, 14, 15, 21, 22n†, 38n, 55, 75, 87, 93n17

dative, 75

deaf, 67. *See also* hearing

death, xv, xxiv, xxviii, xxxiv #24, 8, 9, 29, 34, 46, 46n, 67, 79, 80, 82, 83, 86, 87, 88, 89, 105n12

decision, xiv, xv, xviii, xxvii, 6, 7, 12, 17, 36, 45, 52, 53, 60, 63n†; decisive, 3, 77

deconstruction (*déconstruire, déconstruction*), xi, xii, xiii, xvii, xxiii, xxiv, xxv, xxvi, xxvii, 44, 64, 66, 72n, 92nn7–9, 92n13, 95nn27–28, 95n30, 102n3. *See also* destruction

delay, 75

Deleuze, Gilles, 91n6, 92n6, 94n22, 94n26

Demeny, Paul, 97n16

demonstration, xviii, xix, xx, xxv, xxvii, 5, 14, 18, 19, 20, 21, 24, 25, 34, 36, 41, 49n, 51, 51n, 63n†, 72n, 76, 77, 80, 83, 85, 99n3; *nervus demonstrandi*, 55

derivative, xi, xiv, xxiii, xxiv, 43, 44, 47, 52n8, 63, 83, 87, 88, 93n15

Descartes, René, xiv; *ego cogito*, 36; *ergo sum*, 81; *res cogitans*, 47

desire, xii, xiv, xv, xxviii, 43, 62n, 89, 93nn16–17

destination, 8

destiny, 22, 32

destruction, 10, 11, 12, 36, 56, 102n3. *See also* deconstruction (*déconstruire, déconstruction*)

detour, xv, xxii, 12, 35, 51n, 67, 76

diacritical, 87

diagram, 75

dialectic, xxxii #14, 59

diaphaneity, xv, xxii, xxvi, 66, 69. *See also* non-diaphaneity

différance (*see* xxxiii #22), xi, xiii, xiv, xvii, xxiii, xxvi, 58, 59, 71, 72n, 75, 85, 88, 89, 103n13; infinite, 87

difference, xii, xx, xxi, xxiii, xxiv, 3, 10, 12, 13, 17, 21, 24, 26, 31, 33, 36, 37, 38, 38n, 42, 43, 44, 49, 51n, 55, 56, 58n*, 63n*, 66, 69n, 70, 71, 73, 75, 76, 77, 82, 83, 84, 85, 87, 94n22; indifference, 62

difficulty, 10, 13, 14, 17, 25

disappearance, 46, 79

discontinuity, xxi, 51n, 55

124

58, 63, 70, 72n, 74, 81, 85, 86, 87, 88,
101n2
time, xix, xx, xxii, xxv, 51, 52, 53, 59, 62,
64, 66, 71, 72n, 73, 74, 75, 79. *See also*
present; temporalization
Tomlinson, Hugh, 92n6
touch, 68, 88
trace, xi, xiii, xiv, xvii, xxiii, xxiv, xxv,
xxvi, 58, 73, 88, 103n13
tradition, xxvi, 7, 12, 15, 21, 22, 29, 45,
47, 53, 69, 70, 75, 76, 81, 85. *See also*
heritage; history
transcendence, xxvii, xxix, 66
transcendental, xii, xxiii, xxvi, xxix, xxxi,
6, 7, 8, 9, 10, 11, 12, 13, 14, 19, 25, 25n,
26, 27, 29, 33, 34, 38, 38n, 40, 46, 59,
71, 74, 81, 84, 85, 94n22, 94n26
transcendentality, 9, 11, 26, 68
translation, 15, 63
truth, xii, xvi, xxiv, xxvii, xxviii, 11, 21,
22, 22n†, 25, 26, 34, 36, 46n, 49, 52n,
53, 58, 66, 69, 83, 84, 85, 86, 88, 95n29,
106n14

ultra-transcendental, xii, xxiii, xxvi,
xxvii, 13
unconscious, 30, 53, 54, 54n†
undecidability, xxvii, xxviii, 95n31
understanding, 20, 21, 22, 28, 34, 35, 78
unity, 5, 7, 9, 12, 20, 21, 22, 22n†, 24, 27,
29, 31, 35, 48, 49, 51, 61, 62, 63, 64, 65,
68, 78, 78n, 79, 80, 88
universality, xxi, xxii, 8, 46, 58, 62n, 64,
65, 67, 68
univocity, xv, 45, 80, 86
unnameable, xxiii, xxvii, 66, 72n. *See also*
name

validity, xx, 7, 18, 22, 55, 57, 57n
value, xii, xiv, xxv, xxvi, xxvii, xxviii, 4, 6,
8, 15, 18, 25n, 31, 38n, 39, 46, 62, 66,

82, 83, 86, 93n14, 93n16. *See also* axiol-
ogy; axiopoetic; imperative; *telos*
verb, 62, 63, 64; adverb, 80. See also *logos*
verbality, 21, 64
vigilance, 4, 14, 21
visibility, 29, 33, 61, 62, 67
vision, 83, 88. *See also* provisional; seeing
vocation, 88
voice, xv, xxi, xxii, xxiv, xxvi, xxvii, 13, 14,
19, 28, 60, 62, 64, 65, 66, 67, 68, 70, 71,
88, 89, 94n25, 105n12; *Phonē*, 9, 13, 14,
63, 63n†, 64, 65, 66, 68, 89, 104n6
voluntarism, xv, xxxii, 29, 100n1
voluntary, 28, 29, 30; involuntary, 29, 30
vouloir-dire. See meaning (*vouloir-dire,
Bedeutungen*)

waiting, 84. *See also* coming (*à venir*)
war, 12
west, the, 44; Western, xiv, xv, xvii,
93n15
will, xv, xviii, xxxii, 29, 34, 44, 73, 93n17,
106n14
Wills, David, 92n9
Wood, David, 92n7
word, xvi, xxii, xxvi, xxviii, 3, 4, 6, 14, 15,
17, 20, 21, 22, 23, 24, 28, 32, 35, 36, 37,
37n, 38, 39, 39n, 40, 41, 42, 44, 45n†,
48, 49n, 50, 59, 62n, 63, 63n†, 64, 65,
67, 69, 70, 73, 78, 80, 81, 81n, 82, 86
world, xvi, xxii, 8, 9, 10, 11, 12, 14, 19,
25, 26, 27, 28, 29, 33, 34, 37, 38, 45,
45n†, 46, 64, 65, 67, 68, 70, 74, 94n22.
See also mundanity
writer, 79
writing, xi, xiii, xiv, xv, xvii, xxiii, xxiv,
xxvi, 21, 23n, 69, 69n, 70, 74, 79,
80, 82, 83, 88, 93n16, 99n11; Archi-
Writing, xxiv, 73

Zeigen. See monstration (*Zeigen*)